TRANSCENDING THE I:

A story of breakdown, surrender, and an existential pilgrimage away from the modern world to find my true self.

CAROL A. GROJEAN, Ph.D.

Transcending the I: A story of breakdown, surrender, and an existential pilgrimage away from the modern world to find my true self.

Copyright © 2018 by Carol A. Grojean, Ph.D.

All rights reserved.

No part of this book may be reproduced in any form or by any electronic or mechanical means including information storage and retrieval systems, without permission in writing from the author. The only exception is by a reviewer, who may quote short excerpts in a review.

This is a Non-fiction Memoir

Book design by Carol A. Grojean, Ph.D.
Visit my website at www.CarolGrojean.com

Printed in the United States of America -
First Printing: March 2018
Published by: Sojourn Publishing, LLC

ISBN: 978-1-62747-258-6
Ebook ISBN: 978-1-62747-259-3

The Woodcarver

from The Way of Chuang Tzu by Thomas Merton

Khing, the master carver, made a bell stand
Of precious wood. When it was finished,
All who saw it were astounded. They said it must be
The work of spirits.
The Prince of Lu said to the master carver:
"What is your secret?"
Khing replied: "I am only a workman:
I have no secret. There is only this:
When I began to think about the work you commanded
I guarded my spirit, did not expend it
On trifles, that were not to the point.
I fasted in order to set
My heart at rest.
After three days fasting,
I had forgotten gain and success.
After five days
I had forgotten praise or criticism.
After seven days
I had forgotten my body
With all its limbs.
"By this time all thought of your Highness
And of the court had faded away.

All that might distract me from the work
Had vanished.
I was collected in the single thought
Of the bell stand.
"Then I went to the forest
To see the trees in their own natural state.
When the right tree appeared before my eyes,
The bell stand also appeared in it, clearly, beyond doubt.
All I had to do was to put forth my hand
and begin.
"If I had not met this particular tree
There would have been
No bell stand at all.
"What happened?
My own collected thought
Encountered the hidden potential in the wood;
From this live encounter came the work
Which you ascribe to the spirits."

Dedicated to all soul warriors who courageously seek to change the world from within and who audaciously tell their story to inspire others so they will not go without.

Transcending the I

Contents

Author's Note: Why I Write this Book xiii
Chapter 1: What I Pretended 1
Chapter 2: The Perturbation of My Soul 19
Chapter 3: My Cancer and Dis-Ease 43
Chapter 4: Connecting with Nature 59
Chapter 5: Seeking an Initiation 91
Chapter 6: Fear Kills 121
Chapter 7: My Greatest Challenge 143
Chapter 8: Ayahuasca Teaches Me Love 171
Chapter 9: What I Learned 197

Gratitude

As we express our gratitude, we must never forget that the highest appreciation is not to utter words, but to live by them.
– John F. Kennedy

In 2014, when I severed from the modern world and crossed over the threshold into the liminal space of who I was yet to become, I could have never imagined the journey I would embark upon, the places I would see, or the people I would meet. As I surrendered my ego and begged for salvation, my journey and the following pages did not come because I planned them to be, but rather as a result of the many people who opened up their hearts, minds, and soul to guide me on my pilgrimage.

For my Saybrook instructors and committee leaders, most notably Kathia, Gary, and Alan, thank you for your continued encouragement and providing the direction I needed, especially during those times I was lost. Your support and friendship, as well as instructional guidance, not only kept me moving forward but also greatly helped shape the person I am today. You, as well as several others from Saybrook, each provided me with the tools and perspectives I needed at the time I needed them to learn, reflect, and grow. Your willingness to wander with me on this journey, to challenge me when I was trapped in a limiting perspective, and to support me when I was not able to support myself goes beyond title and job description. I will forever be grateful you were on my side. Thank you.

There are too many people to thank individually, but there is one who I must: Joe. Thank you for letting me go when I needed to leave, thank you for supporting my journey when you did not understand, and most of all thank you for your unconditional love that always opened the door to welcome me home. For my three children, this was all because of you—from the moment I held you in my arms, you represented a sense of joy, wonder, and love that I had lost and could no longer bear to live without. Thank you.

For the many other people whom I was fortunate to meet along the way, for the handful of organizations who guided and shaped my journey, and for the bones who reignited my soul—I have not forgotten my commitment. Thank you to everyone and all.

As eloquently stated in John F. Kennedy's quote above, while my words convey my gratitude, it will be in my next phase, incorporation, where I truly will demonstrate my gratitude for your love and support.

Author's Note: Why I Write this Book

For years, copying other people, I tried to know myself from within, I couldn't decide what to do unable to see, I heard my name being called then I walked outside.

– Rumi

This book originally began in 2014 as an outlet to express my growing dissatisfaction with life—my life in particular. As I began this midlife passage, I quickly realized that the thirst of my curiosity could not be quenched through books, conversations, or spiritual literature and that my urgency for a deeper understanding was beginning to consume me. In a momentary leap of faith I jumped into the world of academia to better understand the world from which I came and how I mirrored it.

The basis of my Ph.D. research arose when I stepped away from the corporate world and shed all external definitions of myself to understand who I truly was and how I had become that way. Not liking what I saw, I sought to change but what I came to experience was how most modern-day approaches to change labored beneath the influence of self-help books, spas, and expensive retreats. It appears that our deepest desire is not to truly to see ourselves as we are, but rather to have someone else tell us where to go, what to eat, or what God to pray to heal our ailing dis-ease. I began to discover how these approaches do not question any of today's underlying assumptions about the modern human's endless thirst for supremacy over, and separateness from, each other and the natural world. Instead, most of these quick-fix solutions merely serve to allay concerns about our personal anxieties, social inequalities, and environmental destruction while, sadly, reinforcing our dependence upon those in power who seek to dominate and control us more effectively.

Transcending the I:

The focus of *Transcending the I* as my research basis was to leverage autoethnography not only as a method of inquiry but also as a catalyst for experiencing transformational change within one person's psyche through research outcomes focused on answering the question:

How can the experiences of contemplative silence, mindful awareness, and indigenous ceremony facilitate transformational learning in support of human growth toward wholeness and interdependence?

Qualitative research is a form of enquiry focused on the interpretation of information based on its relationship to its environment. This subjective perspective differs from the more traditional quantitative or scientific approach, which prefers to reduce an object into parts, facts, and figures for calculated measurement and control. Autoethnography is a specific method of qualitative research whereby the author uses self-reflection and writing to explore personal experience and connect autobiographical story to wider cultural, political, and social meanings and understanding.

While subjective well-being can be hard to define and even harder to measure, the 2017 *World Happiness Report* continues to demonstrate, year after year, that measures of happiness such as economic, social, and health are important to everyone, yet nothing is as important as mental health, or *eudaimonia*, that sense of meaning and purpose in one's life. Through journaling, introspection, and storytelling, I approached inquiry and analysis as a ceremony by which to reveal habits and patterns of my way of being which mirrored the larger culture I researched.

Many findings in my study describe a modern world in need of remembering those sacred bonds of family, community, and a shared humanity. While science has made great advancements in medicine and technology, we continue to fail at establishing a root cause between many of our behaviors and the psychological, physical, and environmental ills of our world. The spirit of my research—and hence this book—drew upon the bases of these practices to demonstrate the power of contemplation, mindfulness, and ceremony as one method of restoring wholeness and relationship within our collective human spirit. *Transcending the I* is the story of my journey and what I learned about myself and my world.

Chapter 1: What I Pretended

People say that what we're all seeking is a meaning for life. I don't think that is what we're really seeking. I think what we're seeking is an experience of being alive, so that our life experiences on the purely physical plane will have resonances within our own innermost being and reality, so that we can actually feel the rapture of being alive.
– Joseph Campbell

After 20 years in a large corporation, I found myself high in the organization chart and earning a healthy income, but unfulfilled in purpose. I kept feeling there should be something more meaningful to life than long hours, with little time for family and friends, full of meaningless things that attempted to satiate my growing discontent. After a few years of soul searching, I realized the source of my discontent was in allowing others to validate my being "good enough" rather than living my own purpose-filled life. I came to see that the collective unconscious within me had become detached from the experience of life and relationships with others, and in its place was the fear and distance I had created toward those things I cherished most.

I yearned to experience life, not be consumed by it. I had no connection to self, to others, or to nature. I was caught up in the rat race, working 60, 70, 80 hours per week and still not feeling this was good enough because there was so much more to do. I was measuring my every moment of life in terms of how much work I could get done. When I woke up in the morning, the first thing I could think about was checking my email—not kissing my husband good morning or eating breakfast with my children, but a race to the computer to be the first to respond, as if to say to everyone else *I'm important, see how much you need me* or, worse yet *I got this, I do not need you.*

Author Robert Bly wrote of how we spend the first 20 years of our life stuffing 90 percent of our wholeness into "the long black bag we drag behind us" and the rest of our life is spent attempting to retrieve it. It is long because it is so full and black because it is our shadow and we cannot see or understand its contents as we walk toward light, and there is no alternative even though it is a part of us, which we are reluctant to acknowledge. This was my plight.

My Story

One day, in early 2014, I sat in my doctor's office pretending to be there for a physical exam, but I was truly there to increase my Lexapro dosage. For the past several years, I had been noticing an increased level of anxiety deep within my gut. It was almost as if the internal beingness of my soul was in conflict with the external doingness of my reality and I was caught in the middle, a third party to my life. My doctor asked me why was I working very long hours in pursuit of more at the expense of happiness in my life and the lives of all those I loved? In a moment of other-world intervention from my earthly consciousness, I told him he was right and that I needed to go on a leave of absence. I am sure that in the moment he saw a glimpse of something I did not, so he took the lead and wrote me a medical letter for leave. Now mind you, I was the sort of person who did not even take vacation for fear of others realizing they could live without me, let alone take five months away from work.

But alas, in my typical way of doing whatever I do with all I have, I took the leave. Not only did I take the leave, but I cut 14 inches off my hair, stopped wearing makeup, gave away my team and job in order to rid myself of all work identity, in an attempt to shed every external definition of myself. No beauty, no role, no title, no meaning to my existence in a society that values what I do over who I am. I sat alone, unidentified in anyway and asked myself *who am I?*

In one of my first acts of being in the world in a different way, I went to Ashland, Oregon to spend a week with a man to whom I had recently been introduced, but otherwise did

Transcending the I

not know beyond a deep feeling that he had something to teach me. This man, who I'll call Sam, was not of this world. We would stay up all night in the most elaborate, existential conversations, which called my soul to sing out in harmony with him. This man was neither male nor female: he was just divine. I have not seen him since our week together and there are days when I wonder if the week was real, other than I believe it to be.

During our week together, Sam was holding a workshop for a local company which agreed to let me participate. One of the activities was an aptly named *what do you pretend?* This activity began by one person asking the person on their right *what do you pretend?* There are no right or wrong answers, just whatever comes to mind. As the question went around and around, the answers became more and more real. Some would eventually start saying that they pretend their marriage is strong, they pretend they are not afraid for their children, they pretend to love their spouse, they pretend they are not overweight or addicted, etc. Eventually the round came back to me and I found myself responding with:

> *I pretend that getting up every morning and getting ready for work, rushing downstairs to check my email to ensure I am "on top of it all" without barely acknowledging my children or husband first. Then I*

get the kids off to school and go to work for ten or more hours, all while sitting behind a desk staring at a screen or in meetings, inside four walls, not even aware of the weather outside, let alone life outside of my small world, arguing for some reason or another and thinking that whatever the subject is, it is the end of the world if I don't get my way. Then I come home late, usually too late for dinner with the family, and plop on the couch in front of the TV, or the computer to work some more, with a big glass of wine to decompress so I can sleep and get up tomorrow and do the same thing again – **I pretend this is a meaningful life.**

As I uttered the words of what I pretended, I remember everyone staring at me as I was asking myself, *Where did that come from?* Perhaps this was me reporting my true experience of life for the first time, rather than just going through each day mindlessly. Perhaps this was a catalyst for me to realize I was unconsciously living a life that someone else framed for me, or more so, that I allowed myself to be framed within, but was not enjoying at all.

Here, in front of a handful of complete strangers, I had a profound realization of all I have been pretending in my socialized, idealistic life. I came to see the cage I had put myself in as I obeyed those social constructs of what it meant to live a good life as a contributing member of society. During this brief, but powerful exercise reflecting my fears, I came to see how the fear I held deeply within gripped me so strongly that it had me sitting every day inside an office arguing with others just to win the argument so I can prove I am more important, that I know more, that I am worthy of more—team, people, money, title, promotion…more love. This fear had me doing all these things rather than experiencing the joy and beauty of life with all the life of this world I came to see during my time trekking the land and helping those animals.

There's an African proverb: "When death finds you, may it find you alive." Alive means living your own life, not the life your parents wanted or some cultural group or political party wanted, but the life that your own soul wants to live. The greatest gift we can give ourselves is being open enough to let others witness our most vulnerable stories; the greatest gift we can give another is to lovingly witness his or her story in a non-judgmental way. From this point forward, I embarked on a journey of change, exploring the world to challenge those ideologies I had so tightly held and to truly experience the world in a way I never knew possible. Initially

I went off to Nepal, Bhutan, and then Botswana to immerse myself in worlds foreign to my own ideologies and my everyday grind of coffee, long hours, wine, sleep, and then repeat. Little did I know at the time that this would be a three-plus year pilgrimage into the depths of this physical Earth and the pits of my internal soul. At my core, I began to question *who am I* if I am not these external labels which show others how important I am and all I have done—my degrees, awards, and more?

What I came to realize was that the story I believed in, that I embraced at all costs to fit in, was not what filled my heart with the love I desired. I was living a life socially constructed and when I turned inward toward myself, toward my long black bag I was dragging behind me, all my values crumbled at my feet. I was left with a big, existential void and the realization that who I was and the life I lived was one big lie.

Parker Palmer wrote in his book *Let Your Life Speak* of how "everyone has a life that is different from the 'I' of daily consciousness, a life that is trying to live through the 'I' who sits inside this vessel." It would appear that there was a great big gulf between my ego wants and my true self, which can only be seen—or more so, heard—by slowing down and listening to that which is not in front of me. He goes on to guide us to sense that running beneath the surface of experience we call "my life," we can find something deeper and more true waiting to become. This isn't easy, and listening to your own life is difficult in a world where we are not taught to slow down and listen to ourselves, but rather to listen to the others, those with power around us.

It appears that my life, my survival, was now dependent on my slowing down and turning inward to listen to what else might be. When people like me are desperate to transform, desperate to heed this inner calling and the urge to die, they need help just as I needed help. Unconsciously I longed for an elder, for that ritual leader, and I longed for ceremony to save me from myself. I needed that guiding hand to show me the necessary ritual to dance, the pilgrimage I needed to trek, and the necessary fires I needed to light so that I did not get burned along the way.

In the act of *severance*, the ordinary, everyday consciousness is challenged, such as when my world as I knew it grew less viable and more morbid. I was driven to change by circumstances in my life such as the death of my parents, the grave illness of my husband, the adolescence of my children, and the separation of my soul from my daily lived reality. I had stepped out into the unknown and now I needed ceremony and I needed someone to hold onto because I could not hold on any longer alone.

For society to survive, thrive even, we each have to be willing to let go of long held beliefs about the way we live and examine our individual impact on the collective whole. For me to grow, however, demanded that I temporarily surrender and be willing to give up familiar but limiting values in which I no longer believed and to let go of relationships that had lost their meaning. As Gail Sheehy wrote in *Passages*, I needed to "take a new step, utter a new word," and realize that what I feared most, the new and unfamiliar, is truly not what I should fear. What I came to realize I should fear is never having the courage to take that first step, utter that new word, and truly experience the feeling of being alive.

In her book *Coming Back to Life*, Joanna Macy asked the question "What are the assumptions and agreements that create obscene wealth for a few, while impoverishing the rest of humanity?" and I cannot help but wonder the same. In 2014, after an emotional breakdown, I set out on a three-year journey into the depths of my soul, and every corner of my world, to experience life beyond the corporate boardroom and frenetic pace of my unfulfilled life of working hard to get ahead. *Get ahead of what*, I had to ask myself, and *at what cost*, as

I bore witness to the state of the world, as well as my soul, which mirrored one another.

My MTV Generation

I was ushered into adolescence with MTV and music videos that taught me that "money for nothing and the chicks are free." My identity as a young woman was instantly front and center on the screen dressed in very little clothing and fronting all she had to other men in an acceptable, if not desirable, manner. I learned I was either to look sexy and be idolized by men or I was going to be shamed and teased by women. As TV became mainstream so did sex, violence, and crime. Striving for ideals such as fast cars, fast women, and fast living in an era of *no pain, no gain*. I watched in horror as my generation mirrored Roman gladiators in their desire, if not demand, to watch violent acts upon ourselves as a form of nightly entertainment.

Desperate to fit in, I entered the work force and saw women wearing androgynous clothing with padded shoulders, so they would look more like men to fit in. Instinctively I knew that I had two choices: either be like a man or dress like a revealing woman to get noticed. I wanted neither. I wanted to be myself but that meant that I would not be taken seriously nor would I be seen—both of which are conditions for achieving success in pursuit of climbing the corporate ladder. Instead I learned how to manipulate men with my beauty, just as I had done with my father all those years, and push away women who competed with me, just as I had done with my mother.

My generation has the privilege of ushering in the cellphone era and with it, nonstop noise and distraction. Always connected and eventually always online, I lost the ability to slow down, breathe, and connect with any other. All my activities were done in the pursuit of growing wealth and material gain to cover my insecurities. In my generation's drive for more, we gave corporations citizenship rights at the expense of human survival. Bigger, better, cheaper, my generation had an insatiable appetite and I thrived in this pursuit. More efficiency, greater economies of scale, and cheaper products through mass manufacturing, all so I could live the American dream. So effective was my *yuppie* (young, upwardly-mobile professional) generation that as our bank accounts rose, we coined the term *disposable income* as if money were something we could spend at-will, regardless of others' lack of even the most basic of human needs. Capitalism gave rise to inequality and the rationalization of *retail therapy* as a form of easing the anxiety from the multitasked lifestyle I idolized.

To accomplish all this, we collectively harvest the earth in a mad pursuit of consuming more while ignoring the devastation left behind for future generations to deal with. My privilege of being born in the Western world was being baptized in the holy water of money, for the ability to capture the almighty dollar became more precious to me than the limited, life-giving necessity of Earth's greatest gifts: clean water and air. So much so that I supported wars when my way of being and access to those fossil resources that fueled my lifestyle became threatened. It turns out that as a nation, aside from being the largest arms dealer in the world, we choose wars that threaten our consumer habits and comfortable lifestyle rather than fighting for the rights of others.

Downing wine, Xanax, and Prozac like candy, and then proudly boasting about my inability to focus because I was so busy, I truly believed that multi-tasking was a sign of a highly productive performer and not a reflection of the growing disease within. *I, me, mine*: I mirrored my generation's cry in a desperate attempt to be good enough and to be loved for who I am regardless of what I do or have. Somewhere along the way, I forgot that love does not come from a mass of things but in my giving of my whole self from deep within my heart. I began to notice how my culture's desperate screams for attention through media and lifestyle were falling onto deaf ears of drugs and alcohol, longer work hours, and a greater alienation from each other. All of this I had been doing through seeking validation in others or running away toward whatever would accept me.

Worse yet, in my frenetic lifestyle, I bought into a social norm that my children were unable to maintain acceptable attention (ADHD) and I attempted to drug them into becoming the domesticated animals their teachers were asking them to be, rather than letting them express the natural human animal nature and curiosity. I watched them suffer at the unease in their bodies from these drugs as I yelled louder for them to pay attention until one day I could no longer ignore their cries. In pursuit of fear that my children might fall behind others, I followed the social norms of introducing them to technology far too early. In this introduction, I soon learned that I could seduce my children with video games and small-screen indoor babysitters, all of which mindlessly distracted them while I continued to work like a slave for my egoic master rather than love and care for my family and community.

Change is an Inside Job

How did I get this way and what prompted me to get off my endless treadmill of ignorance? I am not sure I will ever be able to truly answer this question. The swift exodus that threw me into the liminal world in which I have existed for the past three years cannot be explained in any way other than as an act of pure love, which has been divinely guiding me from the moment I begged and pleaded to whomever would hear my cries. Author Timothy Carlson describes the liminal space as a transitional one; "positioned between states determined by social place, status, maturity, socio-economic position, caste, physical location, mental or emotional condition, health, war and peace, scarcity or plenty." It turns out that life is punctuated by those moments of transitions, that space of ambiguity which lacks form and structure, rather than the dull routines of daily living. What we would do well to heed is the understanding how change is situational; when we change it is not happening to our underlying habits and patterns of our behavior, but rather how we respond to a specific situation or person. When a person is truly transformed, the transformation leads to an inner-reorientation and psychological shift in our core.

My journey changed me in more subjective ways than can be explained or observed by another person. The biggest difference I observe in myself is that my monkey-mind and its incessant chatter, which created a lot of anxiety, apprehension, and fear, no longer occupies my mind and body. Through meditation, contemplation, and time in nature, I have come to see how those defensive actions I held onto for so many years were not about protecting myself from someone else, but rather sought to protect me from those stories inside my head that I told myself about others and my fears of not being accepted or loved for who I am. The reality I now understand is that it was *I* who was not loving or accepting myself and when I closed myself in, I locked in my fears even more, rather than opening-up to let them go.

Transcending the I. I want to tell you that to survive this journey of *transcending the I*, this *I* had to dig deep into her sorrow and regret, which was not easy. My journey had many ups and downs as I went through periods of elation and joy, but it was those periods of depression and emptiness that taught me the most. I came to realize that for me, loneliness was not the absence of company, but rather was the feeling of being disconnected, left out, isolated from others who could hear my story. I was surrounded by family and friends who were familiar with the old me and our modern ways of being, but they were ill-equipped to hear stories of my time on the land, my dreams and visions, or even be able to dialogue with me about the conflicts I was beginning to hold with the very society in which we lived. I went through a few years unsure of my direction, conflicted in what I was doing versus what others wanted me to do, and I found myself depressed because no one understood me. Worse yet, I could not understand myself.

For me, going through these experiences coupled with the ambiguous state of not being who I once was, yet not yet knowing who I was becoming, left me unstable and unsure of the meaning of life in general. I had to dig deep within myself and face my greatest challenge: answering the question *Who am I?* Deep within me I began to see clearly that this *I* is hollow. The *I* is empty and cannot stand alone, for it has no meaning outside of connection with the other, the "Thou," as Martin Buber poetically illustrates in his landmark book *I-Thou*. In my darkest days, I craved connection as I never had before. A survival instinct kicked in for me and I started reaching out to others in a new, genuine way.

I began to see how technology, as advanced as it is becoming to better our world in many ways, was reducing my conversations to shallow sound-bites in a desperate attempt for connection. For me, the internet became a cold, disjointed, false illusion of reality and in my loneliness, I was forced to muster up the courage to dig deep for more meaning of my existence beyond the screen. I began to reach out to people in new and unfamiliar ways, be it knocking on the door of an aging neighbor I'd never known to have a cup of coffee, going out of my way to make a new friend from an unfamiliar face, or staying with complete strangers in a new town to experience life in new and unfamiliar ways. In all this and more, I have found a sense of connection and community I had never known. I learned to slow down and savor our moments together as I no longer look to the other as an object for my leverage, but rather a life-line for meaning and definition of my Self.

The English author D.H. Lawrence believed that people fear new experiences more than anything else because a new experience displaces old, familiar experiences and our defenses or justification of how we define ourselves within them. Just as I experienced walking different lands, meeting different people, and facing unfamiliar and often conflicting ideologies, those new experiences hurt because they required me to stretch and see my old, ignorant Self in a new light. It was only in this conflict between old and new that I could begin to internalize how the external world is no more than a projection of my internal reality. With this perspective, I understand better now how my ego is nothing more than my way of experiencing myself in the world around me. Out on the land and in various ceremonies, pilgrimages, and contemplative silence I came to see how the longer I hold on to false ideologies and dualistic thinking, the longer I will suffer and project my dis-ease onto others. What life asked of me again and again and again was to let go and just let be— and only then could I truly begin to live.

Redemption and Healing

The power of slowing down and stepping out of a task list-driven world is beyond words. Profound encounters such as I have experienced do not come easily, but are well worth the journey and then some. Psychologist Carl Jung once said that coming to consciousness is not for the faint of heart; I could not agree more. While this journey is not one most people could consciously take, it does come when the current path of existence is no longer possible and a person has no choice but to surrender into something greater, just as I did. While I was challenged many times to turn away, what I have learned is that when I stay on the edge of these uncomfortable moments, great growth and transformation toward a new level of consciousness and healing emerges.

Chapter 2: The Perturbation of My Soul

What is necessary to change a person is to change his awareness of himself. – Abraham Maslow

In a gradual, yet epochal perturbation of my soul, I begin my story with the background of who I was, how I mirrored the society from which I came, and what it took for me to finally eliminate the ego of my false self so that a truer, more whole-self could come forward. Mircea Eliade, the well-known religious scholar famous for his interpretations of religious experiences, believed modernity has undergone such a fundamental fall that people today are shut off from any real experience of regenerative space. The result, as cultural anthropologist Victor Turner believes, is the root cause of our social ills or the "fragmented liminality" that pervades much of modern culture today.

Reflecting on my backstory, of who I was and what I lived for, I began to see a person who mirrored her society by striving for meaning and definition outside of herself. Every day, as I pulled further away from my conditioned belief system, I saw how my every act of being, or more so doing, was a submissive worship not of god, but of other people and things to whom I had become a slave. So I pulled back and looked deeply at myself to understand better who I had become and how I had gotten there, to understand who is this *I* in the *Who am I* question.

Bill McKibben, climate-change activist, answers my question best when he says, in his book, *Deep Economy*, "It is perhaps the central assumption of the world we live in that you can tell who I really am by how I live." In my reflection I came to see how I was working very hard for external things such as praise, admiration, promotion, and income, which I only ended up losing myself within. Worse yet, these things did not bring me more happiness, only more loneliness and a greater loss of connection; yet, I was so wrapped up in my life and the gameshow of getting ahead through pursuit of *winner takes all* that I could not see this dichotomy.

My Childhood

Growing up, I had very kind, caring parents and two wonderful older siblings. My parents rarely fought and all three of us kids grew up to be relatively healthy functioning adults by societal standards. We were not rich but we did not want for things either; my childhood was safe, routine, and secure. My entertainment was my father and his shop and I would go out there every night to hang with him after dinner.

Being with my dad was my happy place, for he showed me the love I craved by giving me his time, attention, and letting me know how important I was to him through his actions. Not that I was not important to my mother, but her way of giving me love and attention, as she was taught, was to work hard and provide a clean house and good meals. This is what society wanted of her at the time. To be a good housewife and mother was to provide a clean house and warm meals for your husband and children.

For most of my life, my relationship with my mom seemed uneventful. We did not "fight" per se, but we did not get along either; we were just two very different people (or so I thought). I longed for her love and attention but rarely received it in the way I desired. I don't know why, but I always thought she was trying to poison me. I believed this so deeply that much of my childhood I would not eat the dinner she put on my plate, insisting instead on eating from the refrigerator an unopened tub of cottage cheese, tuna fish, or something else to ensure my survival. Many times I would threaten to run away; once I even packed my bags and sat in the driveway vowing never to return home again. As a small child sitting in the driveway, I secretly ached for her to come outside and ask me to return to her, tell me she was sorry and that she would miss me if I was gone. She did come out, but only to give me some clothes she thought I should take with me. To this day my heart breaks as I can feel my excitement of thinking she is coming to love me, instead meeting with the harshness of her indifference to my leaving.

Real world pressures. Moving into adolescence, I was constantly reminded that the prominent, upstanding people of society were those doctors, lawyers, and businessmen who earned the most money and provided for their family. The unspoken implication was that those who did otherwise were of lesser stature and value to the community. This suggested to me then that the definition of who one is comes through one's role, title, and salary compared to others; that the more you make, the more important you are. Thus, the mantra of my generation was to grow up and be like them. Work was not about following your passion; it was about aspiring to be like others at all costs. We pay the least to those who contribute the most, such as serving the children, sick, marginalized, and elderly in our communities.

As I moved onto college I was lost, directionless and felt I was conforming to a life that was not mine or was not what I wanted—not that I knew what I wanted. For me, college was where I realized the difference between dreaming endless possibilities of what I could be and being told the limitations of who I am. With all this fear about my future, I quit college and ran away, just as I did when I was a child fighting with my parents. It seemed I was destined to be a failure, as my parents repeatedly told me I would *amount to nothing*, especially without a college degree. Instead I was told to grow up and get a life. For my parents' generation *a good life* meant that one needs to work hard and get good grades so they could get into a good college; from there you would get a good job and make good money, marry a good spouse, and have good kids all to one day retire to play and capture rewards of a good life before one dies. I understand that my parents' anxiety and worry about my future came from the experiences of war, Depression, and more—things I had not witnessed—all so I could live in a world whereby many luxuries of their life are offered cheaply at a Walmart today. But somewhere along the way the experience of life itself became a commodity, along with those things I sought to acquire. I began to question a social mentality that defines a good life, as I had, as one who works endlessly in pursuit of more, all to retire into a life of material possession?

I went to work for Club Med in the Bahamas and, after eight months of fun in the sun, I decided to take a job with Continental Airlines while living in Las Vegas and San Diego, each while traveling as much as I could in-between. Come December, 1989, I was broke, lonely, and being stalked in a terrifying way by a stranger. Fueling my anxiety was the realization that I apparently was not doing what others wanted me to do as everyone kept asking me when I would finish my education and get a *real* job. I was 22 years old and decided now must be a good time, despite all my anxiety and ensuing panic attacks, the pressures to conform with what my parents, as well as society, were all too strong to ignore, so I came home to follow their expectations.

First love. As I entered the workforce I met a man so full of life and energy that we connected right away on many levels. About six months into our relationship, Mike* (named changed), who was in the Army reserve, was called to respond to the Gulf war. As he was putting his affairs in order we learned I was pregnant. This was not in my life plan, (not that I had one), and I envisioned being one of those women you see crying on TV because their baby daddy went off to war and never got to meet his child. Gratefully, 24 hours before his deployment, the war was declared over and he never had to leave me. We planned a wedding and got married a few months later followed by buying a home, getting a dog, and having our beautiful daughter. While this all sounds wonderful, going from single to pregnant, married, home ownership and mortgage, getting a puppy, and then having a baby in less than one year was far more than I was capable of handling. Something had to give.

I remember that Christmas holiday in 1992 all too well. Our daughter was a year old and Mike and I weren't talking much. Our marriage was over and now I felt like a complete failure. First college and now marriage and motherhood, a double whammy. I checked out mentally, emotionally, and literally physically, as I ran away to Tahoe for a week of skiing with friends. I was not at home with my family, not working things out, not showing up as a responsible adult; I was just lost and running away. I had no courage to stay in the discomfort of not knowing what to do, which made coming back to face Mike harder than running away. To face Mike and to realize the depth of how much I missed my daughter required me to be willing to see how much I let everyone down in my inability to deal with the pressures of change and growth *all by myself*.

Storyteller and mythologist Michael Meade once wrote that "if the fires that innately burn inside youths are not intentionally and lovingly added to the hearth of community, they will burn down the structures of culture, just to feel the warmth." In my marriage to Mike, what I came to realize was that in my immaturity and lack of ability to see beyond my own needs it was our marriage that suffered. I had been carefree until this point and then, under the weight of all the immense responsibility that came with marriage, home, family, and work, I really needed to start growing up. But who was there to guide my growth and what rites of passage could my community provide to help my transition from youth into adulthood?

An initiatory event occurs when a person goes down a road they did not intend to go down. When a person is pulled further into life than they ever expected to go. When life pulls a person in a direction they would not have chosen on their own. The lack of community to set up a ritual, to hold the container, does not cause the events to disappear. Where culture does not provide initiation, life provides initiation. People have sudden eruptions and breaks in their life that change them from who they were before to who they are becoming. In initiation, a person begins walking the path of the rest of their life by taking the first step of separation, breaking with their life as it was.

Through reflection of my life patterns, I have come to understand that when I hurt and push people away, I hurt and push myself away as well. I see now how I learned to fill the void of disappointment in myself with other things such as working long hours, going to school nights and weekends, and running long distances in-between. I found so much relief in running 10, 15, 20 miles—anything to get this anxiety and angst out of me. I was constantly trying to find ways to push myself to the edge of exhaustion. Anything to make up for my lack of knowing who I am and being able to fill the gap, that void of missing love and acceptance in my soul.

Dad's Cancer

My first experience with cancer was my father's glioblastoma diagnosis and ensuing death in 1999. At this time I was 32 years old and had met a wonderful man, Joe, and we were newly engaged. My career was taking off as I was starting a new role at work coaching and building high-performing teams while being mentored by a fellow from Carnegie Mellon's Software Engineering Institute. At this time, my role was to work with executive leaders of product teams to help them better understand how the struggles and behaviors of the teams within their organization mirror those of the leadership team's behaviors. As if my plate were not full enough, I was back in school receiving my first master's degree. I was on top of the world, busier than ever and full of being loved by the man in my life, by the accomplishments and praise at my work, and by my competency in school.

Then one day I learned my dad was not quite walking straight and something seemed off about his demeanor. My mom took him to the doctor in Portland, Oregon, as we wondered if he had a stroke and I went with her for support. As my father was in the other room getting dressed after a series of tests, the doctor turned to my mom and told her he did not have a stroke, he had a glioblastoma and roughly three months to live, possibly more with brain surgery and chemotherapy, both of which carried huge side effects. A glioblastoma is a rare and deadly brain tumor that doubles in size roughly every week or so.

When my dad was diagnosed with cancer, I remember staring out the window of the doctor's office, pretending not to hear what the doctor was saying. I went numb, could not feel anything, and was inconsolable. Work, school, marriage... and now my father was dying, I did not have time for this. As my father became more sick, I dug deeper into work and school as a distraction to avoid feeling what was happening inside of me. I wanted to pretend my dad was not dying, so I ran away from accepting what I could not control toward that which I believed I could.

Mom's Cancer

One day in 2004, about five years after my father's death, my mom passed out in church. She was rushed to the hospital for tests, which showed that everything seemed fine, but the doctors discovered a small spot on her lung they wanted to explore further. A few weeks later we learned that she had lung cancer but had caught it early.

Due to complications from the surgery and associated medicine, Mom had an abnormally long recovery, spending six weeks or so in the hospital. All this time I worked and was too busy to visit her, unable to feel the pain and suffering of my mother's experience. Joe would visit her often, telling her stories, showing her home movies and just being with her while I stayed home, worked long hours, and finished my second master's degree. Eventually my mom got out of the hospital with a clean bill of health and was feeling good, slowly getting back to her fun life of golf, bridge, and dinner with friends.

A little less than a year later, Mom started to have lower back twinges. A few weeks later I got a call at work, but I was in a meeting, so I did not take the call. Then an email came in from my sister asking me to call as soon as possible, so I excused myself to call her. She told me mom's cancer was back and had spread everywhere, and there was nothing they could do and she was going to die soon. I got off the phone, wiped a tear, and returned to the meeting. Back deeper into work, back deeper into my denial of feeling anything, and back to running away.

The deep pain, perhaps guilt, in reflecting on my behavior and this time in my life is second only to my husband's ensuing cancer. I vividly remember the day I found out my mom's cancer was not a minor nuisance but rather was going to kill her. I was leading a meeting and felt that it was more important that I stay in the meeting, doing my role, than feeling the reality of my mother dying and knowing I am about to lose the last parent I have. I could not even visit, it was too much, and I was too busy. I valued work so much that I'd found more solace working harder than being with my mom. At that time, I was leading a large organizational re-engineering process, performance, and project management effort, which led me to be promoted, managing a multi-billion-dollar project release. As I was winning awards and helping others learn the art of shipping software at the world's largest software company, my mom silently died.

Dr. Martin Luther King wrote a profound sermon while he was in jail for committing nonviolent civil disobedience during the Montgomery bus boycott. In this speech, Dr. King challenges every one of us by asking an illuminating question: "Life's most persistent and urgent question is, *what are you doing for others?*" To which my response at this time was nothing more than working hard and hoping everyone stays out of my way. Clearly for me life was not about relationship, rather it was about what I could control, what I could overcome through hard work, and how far I could run away in denial of feeling the depths of my crying soul.

Husband's Cancer

I would love to hate cancer, for if I were to have any regrets in my life, it would revolve around my behavior as loved ones in my life fight for theirs. You would think watching my father die of a rare cancer and then five years later watching my mother suffer a similar fate would have started to wake me up. Perhaps it did, but I was so far gone that no movement registered on my internal Richter scale. In late 2009, my husband received word that he had leukemia, specifically myelodysplasia syndrome (MDS) refractive anemia with excess blasts, one of the most aggressive and deadly kinds of leukemia. As the doctor uttered the words "he has 12-18 months to live if we do nothing," the world beneath our feet vanished.

At this time our two younger children were 7 and 9 years old and my oldest had just left for college. Adding to the responsibilities of parenting and work, the burden of a full-time sick partner was overwhelming. Once again, as if almost on cue, I was starting my third master's degree and had just begun a new role at work helping lead a once-in-a-lifetime opportunity to be on the ground floor of a brand-new technology innovation. I was confused and scared—feeling sorry for myself for all these cancers happening to me ...*as if!* What Joe needed to survive was a stem-cell transplant, but he could not be a viable candidate to receive it until they were able to (temporarily) eliminate all his premature white blood cells, which were the cancer. While the chemo did its job knocking out the bad blood cells, it took Joe along with it and he ended up spending an entire six months in the hospital for various ailments before his first stem cell transplant. It killed me inside to see this positive, upbeat, generous man so miserable and depressed.

I ended up dropping out of school to have more time with him and the kids, but I threw myself deeper into work as an escape from all this death and disease. Work was the only thing I could control. Moreover, I knew how to be measured and what the definition of success was at work, for they gave me the feedback, love, and acceptance I was seeking. At home, my family, my kids, my husband, and his cancer—I had no idea what to do. I could not help any of them, but most of all I could not help myself. You'd think I'd be grateful not to be the one actually going through cancer and would instead be incredibly warm and resourceful for those I love, yet I have a pattern of doing anything but that and instead I wondered again, *why me?* At this point I did not know how to feel anymore as I was lost and desperate. After all I had been through, watching each of my parents get cancer, suffer and die, I now had to deal with this. *Not fair*, I cried! I checked out, escaped, and I ran away inside my work because here I could escape my inability to help Joe, I could escape my inability to cope with my children's fears, and I could escape my own uncertainties and fears of my life and future.

I see now how I was making the problem worse by feeding Joe's fears of abandonment and by creating fear in my kids of losing both parents one way or another. But I felt abandoned too; first by my parents and then by my husband—and I did not know how to cope. At one point Joe was so angry and in so much pain that I drove him to the hospital and refused to take him home because his trying to stay alive was harder for the kids and me to experience than to watch him die. I felt like I was dying as I wallowed in the death that loomed all around me. Joe was dying though I pretended he was not. Actually that is not true: Joe was living and I pretended he was dying. His dying would have been easier for me to deal with than his living and my having to face my behavior. Joe deserved so much more than I could give and I felt like a horrible person for it. Everyone saw me as wonder woman; I saw a monster who blamed the disease and the situation rather than owning up to her biggest fears. People forgave me, but I could not forgive myself.

Buddhist monk and teacher, Thich Nhat Hanh, warns us that people sacrifice the present for the future, as if a promise or reward of something greater exists at some future point in time if we only work a little harder, give a little more, right now: "But life is available only in the present," he writes. "Walk in such a way that every step can bring you to the here and the now." I was not walking in the here and now; I was running away from it once again. Work was the normalcy in my life through all these cancers and I clung to it more than ever before. I was so scared and sure that Joe was going to die because that was my experience—people left me if I did not run away first to protect myself. Of course, I see now that all of this was an illusion, but I was so lost that I could not see beyond my hurt, let alone how much I was hurting others.

All alone. My children now had one parent in the hospital sick and the other withdrawing into her work. They were overloaded with after-school activities and random people covering for me at night when what they really needed was me to be there for them, demonstrating that they are my priority and that no matter what, we were going to be okay. Sadly, I was not and they were tired from being shuffled around, tired of late nights at the hospital, and tired of this abnormal life they now found themselves living, all the while unsure if their father was going to live or die. As for me, I was not emotionally able to work less; rather, I willingly signed up for more work and justified my actions as being what was paying for his healthcare. From the outside people believed I was superwoman and wondered, admiringly, how I held it all together so well. I was super something, but super woman, mother, wife … I was most definitely not. Perhaps you could say I was super employee, as at work I was continuing to win awards, more promotions, and more responsibility … but deep inside I felt scared and all alone.

What I needed to do most at this time was to recognize my destructive patterns and reorient my heart and mind away from my focus on myself toward the needs of others. Dejectedly, I only felt guilty and was drifting even further into my fear of being left alone. Those six months were a blur; I just remember Joe being very ill, almost dying and struggling to stay alive all the while depressed as hell in contact isolation. He wanted nothing more than to come home and be with us.

On May 18, 2010, Joe received his stem-cell transplant. For all the effort to get to this point, it was rather anticlimactic. A stem-cell transplant looks like little more than a bag of red blood cells for a regular blood transfusion. We sat there, eating lunch, while this new blood breathed life into Joe's veins. Life was looking up, at least until a few days later when I received the granddaddy of all bad news. My dream job got cancelled. I was devastated. *How could life be so unfair,* I wondered? Everything I had worked hard for—my education, my team, my work, and my future—was all gone with the swipe of an executive decision. I had made my work, and everyone within my proxy family, my lifeblood and my support-system to get through each day and now it was gone. I was devastated. No school, no [work] family, sick husband, and now no job. Sure I was employed, but life's meaning as I had defined it was gone. Everything I had built around me, that scaffolding of a life I had created, depended upon, and defined myself by ... was all gone. I behaved as if the Grim Reaper had come to swoop me away. Actually that might have been easier.

I was depressed and eventually took a job in another new venture, trying to recreate what existed in the previous team. Unfortunately, for me this team was anything but that; I was spinning out of control. I started to drink more wine at night to numb myself from the anxieties of my day, from the loss of work and the loneliness and illness around me, as well as within me. All that was my identity and how I defined myself was now gone. I was tired of illness, I was tired of Joe being ill, I was tired of looking in everyone's eyes and being a disappointment when in reality the only person being disappointed was myself. I was lost without a job by which to define myself and I was spinning badly. I prayed, begged, pleaded for something, anything to help me. Carl Jung says "There is no coming to consciousness without pain." *Uncle!* I cried, but something was stirring inside. The pain I endured was loosening a tiny bit of consciousness, awareness, that was about to take hold and help me out of this untenable situation.

I now comprehend how all of this hard work and busyness was isolating me further from what I wanted most—connection with myself and others. My lack of presence with my family, friends, and community was not only hurting them, it was significantly hurting me. Despite all I "gave" to my kids, all they truly wanted was for me to be there and to love them as they loved me. The irony is they wanted from me what I wanted—but could not find for myself. I came to see how all those years of my mom constantly being busy, showing her love to me through her cooking, canning, cleaning, and more, twenty-four hours a day, was a generational cycle I was perpetuating. Her father as an alcoholic and her mother emotionally absent is what she had handed to her and what I was accepting from her. I had to dig in hard and ask myself if I was willing to now pass this on to my children? With all of this new-found awareness I knew I had to change, not just for myself but for everyone around me. But where or how do I begin?

Eventually Joe was released from the hospital to be cared for at home. This was a critical time, as he had few white blood cells and few red. This meant he needed 24-hour support, for even the simplest cut and he could bleed to death or a fever could start and be a full-blown life or death situation within 20 minutes. Our family was now in quarantine: no friends, no extended family, no visitors, period. Joe could not be exposed to anything and if any of us started feeling sick, we had to go away. This was once again a time Joe and the kids really needed me but rather than taking time off from work to help him in these critical days, I hired someone to be with him. I abandoned him; I ran away. I was lost and I was losing my family in losing myself. I was hanging out with people I should not be, taking on more responsibilities rather than being with my family, and I was buying my kids love rather than being with them and just loving them.

Joe was on heavy medications now to prevent rejection of the transplant as well as to prevent any type of illness, be it antibacterial, antifungal, or any other anti-things I had never heard of. He was weak and could barely walk. I prayed for his survival and I prayed for my survival. I was there physically for him, but not emotionally. I hurt as bad as Joe did, and I was scared. I was trying to be there, but I was also running away, pulling away, trying to protect myself from his impending death. I was desperate not to lose all I had worked for and felt that even taking a few weeks off would significantly put me behind at work. Behind what, I have no idea now, but at that time I could not see beyond myself. Lost and not able to focus, I was unable to think.

One more time. A few months later, as Joe was in the hospital for an allergic reaction to some medication, I noticed in a report the doctor handed me that Joe's blood counts had been going down for the past few months. I called his oncologist and they ran more tests only to confirm what I already knew—Joe's leukemia was back.

For this next event, full-body radiation was the entry ticket and the odds were stacked ever more against him. Hard as it is to survive the first round of a stem-cell transplant and all the chemo that accompanied it, survival rates were significantly lower the second time around and there is no third chance. I tried to be there, but I was devastated and started to pull away even further. Initial donor search results yielded no blood match and we were desperate. More drugs, more chemotherapy, more prednisone—all while we prayed and waited for additional searches to yield a donor match.

Joe was angry and scared, understandable for all he had been through, but the prednisone did not help. He would shout, he would be cynical, he would yell at the kids, and most of all he would blame me and yell at me. I knew this was not him but was a side effect of the mass doses of drugs he was on and all he had been through. But the kids did not understand and my heart was broken. The man of my dreams was now someone whom I loved yet simultaneously disliked. It was hard to know who I hated worse: him, his disease, or me. Finally a young man from New Jersey appeared on the scene as a very strong stem-cell donor match and, at the end of July 2011, Joe received his second transplant and began the road to recovery once again. Aside from his overall loss of strength, high doses of chemotherapy, radiation, and year and a half on massive amounts of drugs to keep him alive, he was doing pretty well. His trips in and out of the hospital were much fewer this time around and significantly dropped off after about six months.

Two years of sheer hell. Every day Joe got stronger and was able to do more around the house, taking pleasure in little things like being able to cook for the family or work in the yard. It took a good two additional years for Joe to get fully back on his feet and be ready to look forward to the next chapter of his life. The ordeal was four years total and by the end I could see clearly how much of my inner turmoil was a result of my attitude and behavior.

The more Joe's health improved, the more I became a complete mess. I have heard that when the patient gets well, the caregiver is often left as the "sick" one, and I now understand what that means. Apparently, the chronic stress of daily care for another is a bit of a drip-drip-drip effect that over time has a significant negative impact on the immune system, wiping out the caregiver's defense systems as well as all the adrenals that get you through the day. One study I read said that caring for an acutely sick partner can have the same effect over time on the caregiver as their dying, which is what I felt I had been through. Now, after years of caring and preparing myself for his death, he was alive and well and I felt as if I were the one dying.

With cancer and impending death around me for so long I began to wonder and wait for it to be my turn, wondering if this will be the morning I wake up and find a lump or something worse. What I began to realize was that I already had cancer: it was inside me but I could not see it because this was a different type of cancer. Worse yet, it existed because of me; I had created what I most feared. This dis-ease of my culture was my way of living a frenetic life—overworked and wearing my fatigue as a badge of honor, consuming more than I need and excusing it as approved *retail therapy* while I let the care and nurturing of my children to underpaid, low-valued social workers—was nothing more than how I mirrored my sick culture.

Chapter 3: My Cancer and Dis-Ease

Beware the barrenness of a busy life. – Socrates

As I stared at the bottom of my empty wine bottle, I began to realize that rather than fearing cancer, I needed to acknowledge I have it. I have life cancer, I have a dis-ease of external definition and fear—fear of living life, fear of not being accepted, fear of not getting ahead, fear of slowing down and others getting ahead of me, and fear of what it might feel like to acknowledge my pain. This cancer I had created inside of me had no chemotherapy or other external remedy to heal the wounds. Lord knows I tried with wine, Xanax, Lexapro, and more—anything to stop me from feeling the cancer inside of me. Sadly, all those things just served to fuel it more. My egocentrism led me to the suppression of my passion for life, which in turn leads to a grief too horrible to bear, which I attempted to either run away from or numb through my addictions.

Intimidation, beauty, and intellect were my weapons of choice to combat my life and those were the exact things that were feeding my cancer. So desperate was I for inner peace that I had it tattooed on the back of my neck, as if it were an act of demonstrating to others what I wanted desperately to demonstrate for myself. Not only was this desperate act of anguish tattooed where I could not see it, it was in a language I could not read, either. I was so lost I did not see the paradoxes of my behavior—I was just acting out in misplaced hopelessness for anything to help save me.

My cancer battle had begun and I knew it, but I did not know how or where to begin and my ego mind wanted nothing to do with it. I remember going with a friend to a local Alcoholics Anonymous (AA) meeting in 2014. The impact this experience had on me was far more profound than I could have imagined. There, in that small crowded room with no fancy decoration and where half the people looked as if they had a rough go at it, I witnessed the most beautiful representation of the raw magnificence of humanity. At first I was not entirely sure why I was going. Surely a few glasses of wine at night did not make me an alcoholic, but here I realized that was not what this was about for me. What this was about was my perpetual need to numb myself at night after a day of trying to prove myself to everyone: from my parents (even in death) and siblings, to my husband, my work and my peers. On this day I vowed to no longer blame other people or conditions for my actions. I needed to wake up and take full accountability of who I was as I created my cancer and learned that only I could heal it.

That night, my dream brought a woman who kept telling me *let go of the pain, open the heart… let go of the pain, open the heart….* My cancer had filled me with so much pain that I had closed down my heart and now my survival depended upon my ability to find a way to let go of the pain and to open my heart.

Yoga

When Joe first entered the hospital in January 2010, the local yoga studio was holding community meditation evenings the last Sunday of every month. In one of those divine interventions where you don't have any idea what you are doing, but you do it anyway, I went. The next day, Monday, I went to a yoga class. This was my first time in meditation followed by my first trip to my mat and from there I was hooked. This piece of fabric became my sacred ground and it is where I slowly met myself: I did not like what I saw. I would compare myself to others—skinny or fat, flexible or stiff, perfect or awkward, all while realizing that I am not talking about any of them, I am talking about myself. It was the first time I realized how self-destructive the stories I told myself were. Arnold Bennett once said "your own mind is a sacred enclosure into which nothing harmful can enter except by your permission," and I was beginning to internalize how much my anxiety and lifestyle was a result of this monkey-mind inside of me.

On my mat I had the space to meet my ego and all her attachments. Here is where I met someone who is so busy she doesn't breathe; someone who is so externally focused on job role, title, pay, and level that she is willing to work late most nights and miss time with family or other activities. I began to realize how I cherished work so much I was willing to give it my life. On my mat I could not blame anyone, I could not distract myself (though I tried) and I could not run away from my head or my heart. My consciousness was waking up and was forcing me to face myself head-on. I am a tough agent to be sure, but every day I showed up if only as an act of redemption. Somehow, I knew deep down that my salvation was on my mat and that I had to go there every day for physical salvation, for emotional salvation, for mental salvation, and for spiritual salvation. This was my pill. Not Lexapro, not Xanax and not more wine—nothing was going to help me as much as going to my mat every day. I had so many days where I just showed up and cried, begged for deliverance, and pleaded for something to take it all away. I had been running away from myself and my way of existing through alcohol and antidepressants, but I could not do that any longer. Aristotle said that the ultimate value of life depends upon awareness and the power of contemplation rather than upon mere survival. It was time for me to heed this wise sage.

In class one day the instructor told us a story that was a good metaphor for my journey. She said there once was a bear who was part of a circus and in this circus he did tricks to get fed. One day the circus was on a train to the next town and as they were going over a steep hill, the train came off the tracks and all the animals ran free, including the bear. A day or two later the bear was hungry and started doing tricks in the woods. Slowly the other bears saw him and asked him what he was doing. The circus bear said that he was performing tricks so that he could get fed, as he was very hungry. The other bears fell down laughing at him until one said to him, "Silly bear, you're free now, you don't have to do tricks to get fed, but you do have to feed yourself." The story is a metaphor for what finding myself on the mat has meant to me. I have spent my whole life performing tricks to have someone or something outside of me "feed" me: not just food, but my ego, my desires, my actions, you name it. Coming to my mat was how I was able to know myself; it was where I started to feed myself from within.

Buddhism

As I was spending more time in contemplation of our Western culture and my experience within it, I simultaneously became more cynical about organized religion and fell deeply into spirituality. My quest for knowledge to learn about old traditions of indigenous and mystical ways of being teased me to learn more. During this time, I was introduced to Buddhism and for me Buddhism represented a means of learning to let go of my ego and attachments, surrendering all things of the material world as elements of my human condition. As I learned more about Buddhism and its ways, it spoke to me. I resonated with the notion of not looking for redemption and forgiveness of my "sins" from someone else, but rather looking for the elements of karma and accountability for my actions, good or bad, from within. As Joe was sick, I clung more to my mat and piety for a path out, I somehow knew it was going to be a slow, long journey out of this mess called Carol.

Wisdom of nail polish. I began taking Buddhism classes to learn more about this philosophy. One day, in Buddhist "Sunday school" I understood Buddha's teaching from a profound yet simple lesson. In talking about suffering, or "dukkha," the first of the Four Noble Truths, the Rinpoche used an example of toenail polish. At that time, I loved pedicures and painting my toenails, especially blue, and seeing people's reactions in yoga class. He said, you get your toes painted and you think they are beautiful, but then you start to worry about the polish fading and chipping, as it eventually does. Then you suffer as you try to figure out when and how to get to your next appointment to get these now flawed toes re-polished. You hide your imperfect toes, your mind is preoccupied with the need to get another pedicure, you worry about having the money and time to make this happen. And then it happens again, and again, and again. This is the suffering we bring upon ourselves in the most simplest of all ways. All things around us that we add to our lives, which we use to label, define, or otherwise externally show to others who we are, are all forms of suffering and attachment of our ego. I walked away from that class and have never painted my toenails since. I now cherish the beauty of my natural look and laugh at the gift of this simple, yet so profound, example of what it means to me to suffer.

The more I read and experienced, the more I found a path for myself, a path that explained how I felt and what I was doing to cause those conditions that brought me suffering. Everywhere else I had turned to before Buddhism tried to explain away my behavior and my struggles, but Buddhism squarely put it on me—and this felt right.

Buddhism is said to be the psychology of consciousness, and here I found a safe harbor in accepting my human condition and addictions to all my egos and attachments. This new insight provided me with the reassurance I needed that the inner journey is the right path for me, regardless of how tough it may be at times. I believe fully that it is only through the increased awareness of how my behaviors and attitudes cause my suffering, not anyone else, that I will find a path which offers me peace of mind.

Buddhist psychology is much different from traditional psychology. In the modern world, traditional psychology seeks to strengthen a person's sense of self to help them overcome their challenges or perceived false sense of identity; Buddhism does the exact opposite. Buddhist psychology tries to eliminate self-identity, to separate the self and self-perception as a form of reality. In other words, Buddhist psychology focuses on suffering and the end or cessation of suffering through weakening the grip the mind has on a person, whereas modern psychology focuses on strengthening a person's mind and emotions. In Buddhism, there is no word for emotion or other words relative to ownership, attachment, and emotive responses that give rise to the ego and sense of self. Modern psychology thinks that emotion and condition, cause and effect, are separate from one another whereas Buddhism does not.

Final Nail in the Coffin

After a few years on my mat and my continuing Buddhist studies, I was beginning to see myself, my behaviors and how I was showing up, and the impact I was having on others. Joe was doing great and beginning to work again, and I was finishing my last year of graduate school.

In June 2012, one day after graduating with my third master's degree, I got a call from a human resources leader who asked me if I would be interested in applying for a chief-of-staff position for an "up and coming" vice president (VP). This VP's organization was about to become front line for the company's future strategy in the manufacturing and supply chain division and they wanted to up-level his chief-of-staff role to someone who could help him with his leadership team and organization. I was in heaven; this was the perfect job for me (again!). This new job, I felt, was going to reinvigorate my career and put me back on track for something greater. I was on top of the world again and with this new role I would be working with senior leaders. To that end, I believed I needed to drive a nice car (Lexus), have professional clothes, and hold a particular demeanor—all to play the role I had perfectly designed my whole life for. What could be better for me than this? I won't say all that work I had been doing in yoga, meditation, and Buddhism was *out the door*, for clearly it had a deep impact on me, but my ego came roaring to the front of my intellect and pushed all others aside. What I did not know, could not know, was the war that was about to rage inside of me for the battle of my soul versus my ego. As I was [externally] going deeper into my old entrenched patterns of working long hours and valuing my existence by what others thought of me, my internal soul would have nothing to do with it. I felt as if I were on the end of a bullwhip for which I had no control, caught in-between my two selves who were battling for the death of the other.

Along the path of cancer and illness, work also began "perturbating" my soul. My new job started pressing harder on my old values: requiring longer hours, more stress, more yelling at each other, more blaming each other; I recoiled, frozen in place and unable to move at work or home. *What the hell is going on?* I screamed to myself in the bathroom mirror as I could not move, I could not do anything or worse yet, anything I ended up doing felt like the wrong thing. Work was a monster feeding me, but I did not want that food any longer and I did not feel safe being me any longer. I would react and try something different, then get yelled at for not being what they wanted me to be. This would trigger my bullwhip and I would respond offensively, only to get yelled at again. I would hate myself for caring what they thought of me while I simultaneously hated myself for not being good enough. I felt like a puppet for whom someone else held the strings.

The Buddhist-yogi-mystic-spiritual being inside of me was calling out, crying for me to not fall back in to my old ways, yet my ego needed me to be needed, needed me to have an impressive title and role, needed me to be important. I did not know what to do. More wine in the evening to numb myself, more Xanax to sleep, and now I started on the Lexapro antidepressant to get me through the day. I had to numb myself even more to stop from feeling my soul. I could no longer control my emotions. *How could I have worked so hard to "wake up" and be regressing so poorly?* I conceded, I begged, I surrendered on my mat to whomever would help. Begging someone, something, to take me away from myself. Emotionally I was tormented and confused. I fell further into Buddhism to find a place somewhere with some answers, somewhere I might find my soul.

Incongruence kills. Home was no better. In my ensuing meltdown, all Joe wanted was for me to love him and be with him on his road to recovery and I could not do either. I was still angry at his cancer, angry at his leaving me, and angry at his coming back. I know that anger is a masking emotion; the truer emotion was the sadness I had toward myself for always running away, but I could not face my deepest fears just yet. I was angry at living a life so self-absorbed in my needs to be accepted that I failed to be there for anyone else. I knew I hurt them, but the degree to which I have hurt myself living a life so completely void of loving who I am is an unbearable pain to carry. I had awakened my unconscious and it was screaming at me to pay attention. I was scared of what more it would take for me to truly integrate my internal soul with my external being.

The incongruences I had created in my life hurt, pulled at me, and were killing me physically, spiritually, and emotionally. I was not a whole person, I was a fragmented reality of confusion, anger, fear, and loneliness. I was behaving poorly and I knew it was not okay. Not having control of my emotions was scary and I did not know what was going on. *Am I losing my mind*, I wondered? Perhaps I was truly feeling myself for the first time in a very, very long time. Maybe all the work I had been doing was waking up my soul and, in reflection, that emotional bullwhip was me feeling emotion for the first time from within the depths of my being rather than the rational intellectualization of my mind. But I was scared from not knowing how to manage my feelings and emotions. This was all unfamiliar behavior for me and I found myself lost, yet unable to run away from myself any longer. I tried to pretend this was not happening and worked harder hoping it would all go away, just as I had done all those times before, but it just got louder.

The Calling of Initiation

It was now 2014 and although I loved my job and the people I worked with, the internal cries of my soul had become unbearable. I went to my doctor seeking an increase in my Lexapro dosage for my anxiety, but my doctor looked at me and asked what would it take for me to see how this job and my stress were literally killing me? The implication was not that the company or the job was truly killing me, but rather how I was showing up and what I was holding onto was creating the conditions for my internal dis-ease. I looked at him and after a few moments I told him he was right and that I needed to leave. I'm not sure who was more shocked at my decision—me, my family, or the people I've worked with all these years. Until this point, missing any work for even a family vacation was uncharacteristic of me, let alone letting it all go for fifteen weeks. Now what?

Transcending the I

Initiation into ceremony begins at the moment you feel there is something greater than yourself moving through you. Something beyond just who you are as a name, a member of your family, your role in community: you know it when your current state of being is incongruent with your external state of doing. Author James Hollis says it best when he reminds us that our lives are only tragic so long as we remain unconscious to the growing divergence between the nature of our world and the nature of our choices within that world. Most of the sense of crisis in our lives is induced by the pain of this split.

The disparity between the inner sense of self and the outer becomes so great that the suffering can no longer be suppressed or compensated for. When this realization happens, then de-compensation occurs. The person continues to operate out of the old attitudes and coping strategies, but they are no longer effective. Symptoms of distress should be welcomed, for they represent a powerful imperative for renewal.

But the transit of the passage tends to occur in the fearsome clash between the acquired, socially constructed personality versus the demands of the authentic self. A person going through such an experience will often panic and say *I don't know who I am anymore*. In effect this is true, the person one has been must die to be replaced by the person to be. No wonder there is such enormous anxiety and apprehension to undertake this ambiguous and dark descent. For in this calling a person is summoned, psychologically, to die unto the old self so that the new might be born.

The initiatory journey generally goes in one of two directions. The first direction is an initiation of ascent into the hands of a spirit. With ascent, a person is pulled into great contests, great conflicts, and into great ambitions in order to break out of their existing life and let the fire come through to break open a new one. The other great direction is descent, falling, and breaking down into the depths of their soul rather than breaking out as ascent. With descent, there are periods of loss and a sense of being taken down a labyrinth that seem to have no ending. In these initiations a person does not know where they are, where they are going, or when they will hit bottom. They know only that they are on a road with no map into the depth of the soul.

My journey is of the latter, a steep, dark descent into the unknown. Here is where my quest truly began.

Chapter 4: Connecting with Nature

For money, you sell the hours and the days of your life, which are the only true wealth you have. You sell the sunshine, the dawn and the dusk, the moon and the stars, the wind and the rain, the green fields and the flowers, the rivers and the sweet fresh air. You sell health and joy and freedom. – Hope Bourne

The notion of presence, that beingness of our humanity, has been pondered for thousands of years by many faiths and other practices relative to the existential question of who are we and why we exist. Christians might refer to presence as grace and the workings of God through us, whereas Taoists think of presence as being a shift of subtle energy into one's life force of Ch'i. Buddhists refer to presence as the cessation of the mind whereby normal flow of thoughts ceases and the normal boundaries between self and the world fall away; Hindus similarly refer to presence as the oneness or wholeness of being. Sufis know presence simply as the opening of one's heart. Whatever theology or ideology one believes in, all agree that presence is a felt sense of oneness with oneself and ergo, the world around us, for the world outside of us is nothing more than a reflection of the world within us.

Transcending the I

Man's movement away from living as one with nature toward today's modern society is well documented over the past ten thousand, if not hundreds of thousands of years. In this time there have been many big shifts in human evolution but arguably the biggest shift occurred in our way of thinking when the Greeks came up with the word rational, or *ratio decidendi*, which means the reasoning of a decision as a means of justification for behavior. Starting around 350 B.C., Aristotle loosely declared presence as our beingness in relation to a moment in time, not a state of mind. This began the slippery slope of objective reasoning to things, rather than subjective relationship with others. In the 1600s Descartes took Aristotle's definition one step further by offering the world a break from the Pope and his power to figure out how the world functions beyond God and religious authority. Instead, Descartes viewed the world and everything in it as a machine by literally using a clock as the model of the cosmos and all things within. This notion was then furthered in our consciousness as a belief that presence is relative to time and nature as only a machine within, something that we could then manipulate and control. Descartes' fundamental division between mind and matter, between the I and the world, made us believe that the world could be described objectively—that is, without ever mentioning the human observer. Building off

Descartes and all before him, Newton then further reduced all physical phenomena down to the motion of material particles, which gave us our current belief that presence about *doing* at this time rather than *being* in a moment in time. This belief structure conditions us to assign value to our state of doing in the world around us, creating or making goods, rather than being with what is, as it is, right now. We have devalued the natural world and all artifacts within it as worthless until we humans create something of perceived value from it. We now live in a world where we value time as money and money as love – and we cannot get enough.

This World's Majestic Beauty

Jalāl ad-Dīn Muhammad Rūmī (otherwise known as Rumi) is credited to have said "what you seek is seeking you," though this is an abbreviated translation. The specific language he used stated, "Why should I seek? I am the same as He. His essence speaks through me. I have been looking for myself." For Rumi, the *He* in this proverb is the divine light, lord, and God of our world. Rumi elucidated to us that this God we seek is not just out there for us to worship, it is also within each one of us. I believe by this point in my journey, the God of our greater consciousness that Rumi spoke of, had found me. Not only found me, but was taking control of my life. As I began my journey, I was smacked with the mirror of having to see myself not through the eyes of others but from within myself for the first time as I question much of how I lived thus far.

As noted earlier, my first behavioral act of demonstrating the shedding my old self was to cut my hair very short: 14 inches of beautiful long, blonde hair was gone at the snip of scissors. I also stopped wearing makeup and vowed to live one year in which I had no external definition of myself from my prior life. No hair, no makeup, no job, no title, no salary…no nothing. If, as Lao Tzu said, "a journey of a thousand miles begins with a single step," I had just taken my first one. Me and how I show up in relationship to the other would be how I would come to measure who I am from this day forward.

I decided to next take a walk-about, which is a pilgrimage away from the world as I knew it, to discover something greater about myself and the world I live in. I was drawn to go somewhere that held a spiritual calling for me, somewhere I would walk the land, be in nature, and live among people of a different culture. No hotels or spas; I wanted to get back to the basics of life and strip away everything from the world I had created so as to seek deeply within myself for what might be next. It was February 2014 and I chose Nepal and Bhutan in which to spend six weeks trekking, camping, and immersing myself in Mother Nature and all her glory.

Nepal. As I boarded the plane for Kathmandu, I was excited for the weeks ahead—six weeks being completely out of my normal day-to-day schedule, days where I have no roles and responsibilities besides getting up every morning to hike and pitching a tent every night to sleep. For the first time in decades there were no computers consuming my attention, no emails demanding my reply, no calls needing my answer, no meetings to attend, and no one to parent or to answer to. A month and a half of pure self-reflection and time in nature with my only accountability being to just show up and figure my shit out.

Kathmandu is like many over-populated third world destinations with crowded streets, little to no lane definitions in the roads, and people and animals everywhere. A hustle and bustle of a different style of life. The closer you get to the city, the narrower the streets get until you are between two buildings on a street that is more like a packed one-lane dirt road where you negotiate space with an oncoming car, tuk-tuk, or bicycle. I spent the first few days in Kathmandu getting acclimated to the time zone and elevation changes. Here I met my trekking partner and in these days we traveled to Nepal's ancient capitals of Patan and Bhaktapur to visit sacred Hindu and Buddhist temples, meet the Hindu monkey gods and other holy men, as well as watched sacred ceremonies for the burning of the dead on the banks of the Ganges River. I was in heaven with all I was taking in, as I had never experienced anything like this before.

A few days after arriving and getting acclimated, I met my guiding team and we drove to our trekking start point, the small village of Gorkha, to immediately begin our trek. From the first moment I began walking, I knew this is where I needed to be. My soul sang and my eyes could not take in enough of the beauty. If past lives do exist, surely this is where I came from. For our first night we did not trek too far, because we spent most of the day driving. We pitched our tents just over the hillside from Gorkha and began making dinner. What I noticed right away were the kids, who were all outside until complete darkness, running around playing with whatever ball or dirt piles they could find, and they were having a blast. They had no electricity, no indoor plumbing, no iPad, computers, TV, or other distractions to pacify themselves. They literally had almost nothing, yet they were having tons of fun running around, getting dirty, and living life.

When I opened my tent flaps that first morning and saw the splendor of the Himalayas spread out before my eyes, I wept. I wept for all the years I spent inside four walls hoping someone would notice me. I wept for all the anger and hostility I created in arguments that were over nothing but my ego and stature. I wept for the busyness of my life in pursuit of tasks and activities toward goals, products, and services, which added no value other than to further my alienation from this majestic world. I wept because for me to live my life, this is what I was looking for: the simplicity of returning to almost nothingness and to see the beauty in my surroundings. To see the beauty in the people, the earth, and her majestic mountains was all too much for me to take in.

To think for one moment that I could have lived my life without witnessing the beauty of the Himalayas, without experiencing this world and all her glory outside the four walls of a corporate boardroom, was more than I could bear. I have been told that crying for yourself can heal deep wounds. This is not the same as feeling sorry for yourself, which happens when the ego is in control but feels helpless; rather this is a cry that comes from the heart, for the heart cries for us as we recognize our wounds, our human limitations. This moment truly was a transformational time when all my beliefs and values were called into question and I could do nothing but weep with a cry that came from my heart as I recognized how wounded I had become. A Sufi verse says, "When the heart weeps for what its lost, the soul rejoices for what it's found."

This was my experience in Nepal. The regret I came to realize was a result of the past two decades where I have put my career and social stature above fully living. Gratefully, this sorrow was also met with a rejoicing deep in my soul to have experienced this new, first breath, and to finally be waking up. Psychologist Carl Rogers once said that the process of the good life is not a life for the faint-hearted: "It involves the stretching and growing of becoming more of one's potentialities…the courage to be. It means launching oneself fully into the stream of life." Here with the Himalayas spread out before me I felt myself grow!

For the next 16 days I trekked 8 to 12 miles per day over many hills and through many valleys all throughout the Gorkha region. With each and every day the scenery became impossibly more beautiful, as well as did the people. At every village I was greeted by its people who were always very kind and gracious. Despite their having very little, they brought everything they had to share with me: walnuts, mandarins, and fresh farm eggs. I was floored at their generosity. I barely know my next-door neighbors, let alone welcome strangers and offer all that I have, but here these people open up their entire lives and possessions to share with me whatever I might need.

Desperate to learn. Most every village we trekked through had some form of a school for village children, even if they had to hike miles to attend, and even then most kids came to school hungry and received little or no food while there. Most of the schools I visited were constructed by the adults in the village because the government rarely provided much food or supplies to remote regions. These buildings had just one opening that served as window and door, yielding no protection from driving winds and snow. Inside, the children were lucky if they had plank desks and hardened mud or old wood benches, as 15 or so children of various ages gathered around the one or two books they shared amongst themselves. It was a disheartening sight to see until I saw them during recess on the playground, running around and happily playing with nothing more than a stick around a bicycle-tire frame, or something of that sort, trying to keep it rolling while the others chased it.

Even hungry, they seemed happy enough. It was mind-blowing for me to experience, once again, such pure joy despite their lack of modern world conveniences. These children were extremely polite, eager to learn, and wanted to learn as much as possible from me. I came to see how much I suffered when these children suffer. Perhaps suffer is the wrong word, at least you would not see that word in their expressions. But I sensed inside of me a growing suffering that was not based on my lack of resources, but on theirs. I began to realize that they and I are connected, that I cannot exist in a world and be a whole person as long as they (or any others) are not getting their basic needs met.

Bono, lead singer of the band U2 and active humanitarian, spoke openly at a Georgetown University global social enterprise event in 2012 on just what I was experiencing. He stated that when you truly accept that those children in some far-off place in the global village have the same value as you do, your life is forever changed: "You see something you canot un-see," he said, and this is what I began to internalize. It was as if a large whack of humility rang throughout my body and I became more aware of my perceived lack of having not enough in all my material wealth and privilege. *When did I become so arrogant and disconnected from what matters most*, I wondered to myself?

Celebrating life. One of the most remote villages we visited was Siran Danda. It was incredibly beautiful and I swear if I reached my hand out far enough, I could touch the Himalayas. When we arrived, the village people were preparing for a celebration as they had just received running water into the village. Not into their homes, not warm water, but simply cold running water to a central square of this small village, which was the home of no more than 50 people. In preparation for the big celebration, the women were busy chopping vegetables and potatoes while the men prepared a goat for the feast. As the adults prepared the meal, the children ran around collecting rhododendron flowers and then showered me with them. I felt so warm and loved inside. They expected nothing from me, wanted nothing from me other than to just be.

Again, what I perceived as lack, they saw as bountiful and were so grateful that they prepared a celebration for this wonderful attainment. This was another one of those moments where I felt put in my place, wondering *who am I* to complain about a bad cup of coffee, traffic, or any other condition I create in my "first-world" problems when these people can celebrate gloriously for something as basic as access to water. I struggled at the simplicity of their existence and the joy in their eyes. This was all I had ever wanted in my life, and if it was so simple to achieve, why did I work so hard for so many years? Why are so many in my culture literally killing themselves to get ahead in a rat race for which we all know how the story eventually ends? I began to see the way I was living life was as if I were in a mad pursuit for a prize at

Transcending the I

the end, my death, rather than the enjoyment of the journey, my life, itself. I kept wondering, how could I have lived a life of such insanity for so long? How can we all collectively keep denying our interconnectedness and the beauty of our world we are simultaneously destroying in our pursuit of more?

Soon the celebration began and I stood to the side, taking pictures of their beauty and witnessing the joy in their communion and singing. One woman noticed me and made a gesture that I took as asking me if I wanted anything. Not wanting to offend, I nodded yes. She brought me a glass of liquid, which I thought was water, so I took a big gulp only to realize it was Raksi. Raksi is a strong drink made from millet. It is clear like vodka and tastes somewhat like Japanese sake—strong! I'm not sure what look I had on my face as I realized this was not water, but the whole group started laughing at me. I am sure it was quite funny. They motioned me to join them so I went and sat with the whole group as if I were one of them. They did not judge or fear me because I could not speak their language or looked different from them—that did not matter. They walked around and plopped a large pile of rice, potatoes and tomatoes, and goat meat onto my plate as we ate with our fingers. It was hot and delicious and I loved being there among their beautiful community. How they came together and connected, shared with each other whatever food they had, as well as with me, and laughed and sang together had me realize how alienated I am from my community.

All too soon my trek in Nepal came to an end as we finished up in Pokhara, the second largest city in Nepal. This day was also a deeply religious day for Hindus around the world, though all peoples of Nepal gather for this celebration. Known as Holi, the festival of color and love, people all over the country celebrate by partying and throwing bags of color all over everything, and everyone, around them. They play music and dance in the streets, and you cannot escape getting pulled in and colored yourself. It was hilarious and amazing to see so many people having so much fun. One of the many things I adore about Nepal is that people may come from different religious backgrounds, but they all respect and appreciate each and every one. On this *Holi* Hindu holiday, every person of every religion was joining in the fun. There was no discrimination, no judgment, no "us versus them" – there was just *we* and we celebrated big!

Bhutan. After a few more breathtaking days my trip to Nepal came to an end and I was off trekking in the land of the Thunder Dragon. My first trek was a short, but oh so very steep, three-mile climb up to Tiger's Nest. Tiger's Nest is a prominent Himalayan Buddhist sacred site built in 1692 in

Transcending the I

the cliffside of the upper Paro valley of Bhutan. It is one of the most photographed places in the world and to see it in person is beyond words. I was invited into a few rooms to witness prostrations, sacred objects, and admire the various deities and other sacred objects that protect the lands of Bhutan and its people from greed, arrogance, hatred, and the sort. I wondered how I could bring this all back to America.

Bhutan was different from Nepal in many ways—from the architecture of the buildings to the royal monarchy oversight to the well-stocked schools whereby all kids are clothed, educated, and fed all the way through college. They are very much a community where no one goes hungry and there is no such thing as homelessness, as everyone is cared for. Not that Nepal and its people do not care, but the impact of each region's history and leadership have yielded a much different outcome in many ways. I suppose much of the biggest difference comes from their population sizes as Nepal has about 28 million people, whereas Bhutan has only 770,000. This was evident in my trekking. In Nepal I frequently came across villages daily, in Bhutan I could go a few days and see no one.

About this time I began noticing how I had slowed to a pace of being, a presence about me, that was new and unfamiliar. Perhaps this was because I had been removed from the daily routine of my life and all my busyness within it for a few weeks now. I remember one day in Bhutan, I sat in a meadow and started looking at the hillsides in front of me and sky above me. I began seeing images of animals and faces of people everywhere. I started making up stories, which I also believed, that these entities truly existed to protect that land and its inhabitants. I loved learning again how to be childlike in my joy and pleasure of seeing images in things and pretending, being curious and open to, what if…I would look at the clouds and see the amazing shapes, more faces and animals all swirling above me. I hadn't done anything like that for so many years. Just a few weeks earlier I would have deemed this activity a waste of time, assuming I would have considered it at all.

In Nepal and Bhutan, as I experienced children running around with very little, yet experiencing so much joy in life, I began to feel a pain my children must have in their souls from being locked inside our house, addicted to video games, YouTube, and texting with friends. They don't know how to spend time outside playing or being creative without the distractions of a screen or other form of entertainment in front of them. I wondered why I created these conditions for my children? What society would believe that bringing children indoors, plopping them in front of screens that often portray acts of violence and prejudice at worse or mindless numbing of the creative brain at best, would yield a happier upbringing than the scarce conditions such as this? I understand that many children in Nepal suffer far greater with their lack of education, health, and food security, but they do not let that stop them from enjoying life and they certainly do not walk around pouting or throwing temper tantrums so, why do we? In my society we teach people to hold on to all that they have, not share it with others because it could all be gone tomorrow, yet we simultaneously spend our excess money (disposable income) on meaningless things we would be better off without. I can't help but wonder why we continue to let this happen. Don't we see the hypocrisy even in our vocabulary? I read that one-fifth of the world consumes four-fifths of its resources and I see the impact of my one-fifth on these people around me. Our world contains more than enough of what we all need to survive, if not thrive.

Botswana. In early May 2014, Joe and I were talking about a friend who had been recently diagnosed with lung cancer. She was one of a handful of people who had received a cancer diagnosis in the past year; we were reflecting on how short life is and our increasing value of the need to fully experience and appreciate life every day. Around the same time we had this conversation, we were also reading about endangered species and how our children's children may never see some of the species that exist today (e.g., rhinoceros, elephants, etc.). Joe had spent a few years in Africa in the Peace Corps and he was particularly waxing on how he wanted our children to see these beautiful animals before it was too late. My leave was coming to an end at the beginning of June, but I had originally planned for four weeks of vacation time in July and I intended on still taking it. After a long discussion, we decided that I was going to take our daughter, who was just turning 14, to Botswana for the month of July. This would provide me quality mother-daughter time before she entered high school; saving the animals is one of her driving passions and I longed to continue my quest inward in any way.

In July 2014, we boarded a plane for Botswana where I would find a world even further from my experiences thus far. Fourteen of us resided for five weeks deeply immersed in the savannah of the land with only a gathering shelter and fire pit. With no running water or natural food, we had to cart in what we needed as the nearest village was a two-hour drive away. Here no fences or walls protected us from the animals, or vice versa, just the skies above and the expansive savannah all around. This was not a retreat; it was work, and over the course of those five weeks, I learned how to restore the land back to its natural state, build watering holes to retain water for the animals, and track and monitor the various birds and wildlife to establish their presence, progress, and health, and much more.

Here my daughter and I came face to face with hyenas, giraffes, elephants, and so much more. It was as if I had been transported to a realm of existence where animals, not humans, ruled the jungle, and I was there to witness their majesty on their terms, no bars or cages. When you slow down enough to listen to the world in a different way, it talks to you. I had two particular occasions for this: the first was when we were sitting atop a hill on rocks. Sitting there enjoying the view, I heard a voice tell me to move, that a black mamba was near. A black mamba is a deadly, venomous snake. I decided to heed this inner knowing and move somewhere else, within a few minutes another person screamed and pointed to where I had been sitting, and sure enough, a black mamba was slithering across the stones. The second occasion came on my birthday; as I entered my tent I found a small leather pouch with an OM symbol amulet inside. No one on the compound had given this to me; it had just appeared and I knew that it was a gift of healing and protection for my journey. While these experiences may not have been overtly profound, many of my experiences such as these were the tiny rewards captured for having the courage to lean in and be open to what else might be possible.

Animal kingdom. Botswana for me was similar to Nepal and Bhutan in terms of continuing to find myself and connecting with nature, but in geographical terms it was much different. While the land and people were also very warm and beautiful, I came to understand how our arrogance and greed in treating the land and her resources as our domain have destroyed not only this beautiful terrain, but the animal spirit within it. These wild animals are so big and beautiful but I could feel the fear inside them, see how they are scared of us as a result of how humanity has come to treat them as objects for our entertainment or trophy case, rather than subjects who live with us in one world where all lives are respected. The widespread domination and control of nature, such as I witnessed here in Botswana, is implicated in the deterioration of the human psychological, social, spiritual, and environmental realms, particularly of the Western culture and ideology.

In my slowing down into silent contemplation as I lived off the land, I was able to hear these animals. They helped me see that when I limit my life to the daily grind of task lists and to-do's in an organized march of expectations from the whole, I was the one who became the caged animal. Out in the bush I was on land that civilization has yet to domesticate for its use and I could feel the raw and primal sensation of truly living. The stars shone brighter than I had ever seen before and I was taken back to days when people still were at one with the earth and cherished our connection to nature's cycle. Spending time in Botswana opened my eyes to the role each life form plays and the delicate balance in which we all coexist.

What does it Mean to be Human?

Existentialism is a philosophy that focuses on human existence and the dramatic survival and flourishing of living on the stage of a human's life. This modern philosophy believes that it is in the gift of being human that one has the retrospective ability to understand life as transient and that we all die sooner or later; however, when or how we die none of us know until the final hour. And it is in this awareness of our eventual death that leads many humans, such as myself, to ask existential questions such as:

- Who am I?
- Where did I come from?
- Where am I going?
- What is the purpose or meaning of my life?

By design, life is an ongoing identity crisis of the self to define and redefine who we are as we go through many of the major transitions and upheavals experienced over the course of being alive: adolescence, adulthood, parenting, divorce, middle age, retirement, loss of job, death of loved ones and more. Psychologist Daniel Levinson wrote in 1977 about the seasons of a man's life and how each period is marked as being a stable period, until it is not, and then it is a transitional period. A transition in life is a tremendous opportunity, when acknowledged, for self-redefinition and inner reorientation of who you are from who you once were. Throughout our lives there are equally important transitions, as well as life events, that are also worthy of recognition and require our attention. The stable period is the time when a person makes crucial choices in life, builds a life structure around these choices, and seeks goals within the structure. The transitional period is the end of one stage and the beginning of a new one.

Regardless, at some point in life, whether triggered by a major turn of events or misfortune, a disillusion with the emptiness of success, or merely feeling bored in one's life, the existential question of meaning will be triggered. This is largely in part because it is our nature to live fully present and oriented with a purpose toward something greater than ourselves. We inherently desire to do something significant by which we will be remembered for when we are gone, otherwise what is the point of living?

I quickly learned on my journey that my worse fear is not death, but is the discovery that I never really lived when the time comes for me to die. To think I possibly wasted a moment of my precious life not living to my fullest potential is a greater fear than the fright of dying alone. I began to realize that my fear of death is not in who I leave behind, but rather is in how will those I love remember me? Did I want to be remembered as a person who worked non-stop as her form of love, who bought others' acceptance of her beingness through monetary objects, and who could not sit alone, misidentified as anything but those external labels she put upon herself to hide her truer being in the world? No, I came to see that the way I had been living would have yielded the most regrettable life I could imagine upon my death bed.

The ancient Delphic injunction carved into the lintel at the Temple of Apollo reads *"Know Thyself."* This was inscribed some three thousand years before Christ, yet still resonates with many people today. Without a clear sense of self-inquiry, we can go through life without ever knowing who we are and what we really want out of our life. The German philosopher Heidegger refers to this as non-authentic and authentic modes of living. Non-authentic people give up their individuality and responsibility for the security of being part of a herd. In contrast, authentic people assume responsibility to live in a way that is consistent with their true nature and core values. They strive to become what they were made to be in spite of anxieties and risks involved.

The challenge for each of us is that we cannot buy our authenticity and there are no shortcuts to this inward pilgrimage to get to know one's self. The process of authentication begins with a deep knowing from within that there is something inconsistent with the way I am living my life—the very core of my being, rather than my doing. When this calling came for me, there was a moment of awakening to this awareness followed by a deepening inquiry into my core values and a felt sense of identity aligned to my true beingness.

It is the discovery of an inner vision about my uniqueness and singularity that endows my life with deeper meaning. But how does one begin this journey of self-inquiry? While the specific instigation for this beginning is unique to each one of us, the quest to discover oneself is universal in that it begins with discomfort in sensing a lack of authenticity in one's life. Sadly, few heed the call because social pressures of conformity create defense mechanisms within ourselves to keep our anxieties at bay, and socialization provides us an easy escape from the existential quest. Canadian psychologist Paul Wong wrote, "The dehumanization in a competitive capitalistic society further narrows people's vision to material gains. As a result, people are confused about their true identity in the larger scheme of things. Thus, the quest for authenticity remains a challenging and poignant task in a consumer culture." All of this prevents us from experiencing our self in the world as the world is, not as we think it should be.

The quest for authenticity, that peak experience to achieve one's highest purpose, is not for the faint of heart, nor is it always compatible with the pursuit of happiness and living the "good life." The stories of Jesus, Socrates, and many others have taught us that to live an authentic and meaningful life means that one cannot deny his/her true nature and calling, even if it means death—psychologically or literally. There comes a moment in the death-resurrection experience in which there is a shift from doing what we know will sustain us to allowing ourselves to be sustained by the greater of us all. But as the hero knows all too well, the greatest journey of all is the road back home. Known in many indigenous ceremonies as the *incorporation* phase, it is only by bringing the lessons and wisdom back home to your people that the entire journey itself merits any meaning and value.

When you have accomplished all this and can now help others, you have lived a full and meaningful life.

Feeling the Heat

In November 2014, I participated in my first sweat lodge while in Sedona, Arizona at a book-writing retreat. As I was reaching into the depths of my soul, I felt I needed to build upon these experiences through this indigenous ceremony so as to call upon my ancestors for their wisdom and my salvation. As we were nearing our location I could see the fire burning in the yard. Off to the side was a small, specially built celestial sweat lodge. Today was not only a great opportunity for me to participate in this event, it was also a trifecta day with three cosmic events—a solar eclipse, a super moon, and the spring equinox. Aiding to the mysticism of this event was that all participants, apart from the leader, were seven women ranging from 20 to 80 years old.

The sweat lodge seated eight of us cozily around a fire pit in the middle. There were eight points to the structure, each representing four earth directions and four spiritual directions, and it was covered with thick black plastic and blankets to keep the darkness and heat in. The person who leads the ceremony is known as the water pourer; this is the role Bear-Cloud held. He began by placing four hot rocks around the center, one for each direction; and one in the center as the embodiment of our ancestors, our grandfathers and grandmothers, each of whom are passing along their wisdom to us through visions and insights while in the lodge.

The first round represented the Eastern door, the door of the sun rising, yellow in color. Bear-Cloud placed seven hot rocks into the circle followed by some herbs which initially lit up like stars to summon our ancestors. The door closed, the heat rose, and it was pitch black. Bear-Cloud began with a Native American song and we sang along with him as best we could. He began by speaking about the significance of the Eastern direction and how it represents life: how the daily rising and setting of the sun is symbolic of the ebbs and flows of life, and that it takes these ups and downs in our lives for us to understand balance and harmony.

After a bit more talking and another song, Bear-Cloud added seven more rocks and began in the Southern direction, of the Earth the realm, red in color. He taught us about how the Earth is covered by scary looking serpents and spiders, who live closest to the ground as their role is to protect Mother Earth. Additionally, he taught us how the snake sheds its skin to remind us every day how we can begin anew, that we have a choice to shed our yesterday selves and begin again today or not. Bear-Cloud also spoke about the worm (worm nation, he called them) and reminded us they are also sacred (as are all animals) because they breathe life into the earth, constantly turning it over to keep it healthy and organic, just as we should be continuously cultivating our lives. By the end of the second round I was sweating profusely, but hanging in there.

When life gets too hot. Time for the third round and another seven rocks, a total of twenty-one now. The third round is often the hardest round because it is represented as the dark, evening realm of the West. This is when our shadow sides appear, and it is also where we break down mentally, physically, emotionally, spiritually—all of which I did. The third round is about the door to the underworld protected by the bear and the lightning spirit. The bear is a good example for us because it is able to hibernate for the winter, go into the darkness all alone, and endure during dark and lonely times. I tried to think about this as I was beginning to have a panic attack, feeling unable to breathe in the thick, hot air all around me and made worse by the unrelenting darkness.

I honestly did not know if I would make it; the thought of death or losing my mind was a constant negotiation, so I reached out to touch those around me to remind me that my sisters were there supporting me. I kept my eyes closed and meditated on the Buddhist mantra *om mani padme hum* over and over as I begged to invoke the powerful and benevolent blessings of Chenrezig, the embodiment of compassion. I was thanking my ancestors, my parents and grandparents, all those who have gone before me and begging for their grace in my salvation. As the heat continued to rise, I continued begging, not sure I could make it.

About a quarter of the way into the third round I got onto my hands and knees and then quickly dropped to the ground in a desperate quest seeking the coolness of the earth. This provided me with a brief respite, but minutes later my mind caught up with me and I found it hot again and too hard to breathe. Every second in that moment was an eternity and I was in an internal dialogue of negotiation with my mind to hang in, not to panic (too late), just keep breathing and remember I am a spiritual being in a physical body and not the other way around. As the heat continued to rise, every cell in my body was pulsating and I could feel the fragility of life inside of me. I was soaking wet and my breathing was shallow as I begged Mother Earth to save me. I was acquiescing to all things, I was suffering and willing to release all ego, my ego was completely banished and I one-hundred percent let go, begged for my life, and simply surrendered to whatever there was to be. I surrendered the final bits of my soul that remained and begged for forgiveness from all whom I have hurt.

The round eventually ended and Bear-Cloud opened the door oh so slightly. My panic slowly subsided as he talked to the group about the Chanupa, the sacred ceremonial pipe, and passed it around for all of us to smoke as a practice of sending our prayers straight to the ancestors. By the time it got to me I was able to take it, grateful to be alive and thankful to my ancestors for all the wisdom I had received. Gratefully, the fourth round was much shorter and less hot than the third and with the sweat culminating in a break-fast, I celebrated my survival with a thanksgiving for the ancestors.

Learnings. The ancient tradition of a sweat lodge was a perfect initiatory first ceremony for me. As I began my journey toward pursuing personal self-transformation in support of my growth toward connection and interdependence, what better way than cleaning and purging of my body. A sweat offered my mental body an opportunity to face my fears of death head on, to clear my mind of idle distractions and increase my mental clarity; the sweat offered my spiritual body a time of contemplation, introspection, and connection to the spirit world and its ancestral wisdom—awakening me to a world beyond all I see with my eyes; and the sweat offered my physical body the cleansing of those wounds and toxins which cloud my ability to be present, enabling me to free my body of the dis-ease and ills it continued to carry within.

Most of all, this sweat lodge was such a great representation for life for me! There are ups and downs, hot moments and moments where survival is in doubt in my life, but with a community around me, supporting me, and helping me through the tough times I was able to endure and because I did, I came out a better person for it. I have often heard the axiom of how we often think that holding on is what will make us stronger, but in reality sometimes is in the letting go where our greatest growth occurs, and never was that truer than in this moment in the sweat lodge for me. What I learned from this sweat is the power of letting go and leaning into my greatest fears because more often than not, they surprise me in becoming the greatest gifts I've ever received.

Motivational speaker Wayne Dyer liked to say that life is one big leap into the abyss, the unknown depths of our soul. One where most of us grab ahold of a rock as we go down, hoping to control something or find something solid we can call ours so we are not alone. When in reality it just weighs us down as time, like those material possessions we define ourselves by, passes by more quickly in a crash of our ensuing and ill-prepared deaths. Here, as I was clinging to my life and about to lose myself, is where I first learned to let go and in this act I was truly able to breathe for the first time in a very long time. Little did I know at this time how this would be a metaphor for so much of my journey in the next few years.

Chapter 5: Seeking an Initiation

The characteristic mark of substantial change is that the object undergoing the change does not survive that change or persist through it, but is destroyed in the process. – Aristotle

The world of progress with its all-consuming tendencies is essentially a world that feeds on anything that lives, turning the human into an indentured servant fed with material things, yet starved for everything else. In this context, ritual is the return to the ancient with a plea for help directed to the world of the spirit. A modern seeker of ritual, such as myself, acknowledges that I am wounded and have been emptied of all vital substance to the point where I am disgusted with the present state of my life. Tired of being enslaved to my way of being, I sought a ceremony with the ancestors that was deeper than a sweat lodge and more life-altering than a pilgrimage. I needed to speak with the ancestors to witness that which is greater than I am, and to feel the love of my mother.

During my journey away from the modern world, I came to deeply question values I had held since my youth to discover, more deeply, what values and beliefs I now hold for myself. The core question became *what is true for me*, as I sought to separate from the herd mentality, just as Zarathustra's camel did for Nietzsche. I have come to learn that it is only when the initiate is ready to die, to let go of what no longer serves, whether that be the clothes off one's back, material possessions, or old ideologies, is a person truly ready to grow. Anthropologist Piers Vitebsky declared, "The initiate may see him- or herself as a skeleton...every bone and muscle is taken apart, counted and put together again, while blood oozes from the joints and the candidate's inert body as it lies in the tent," Sacred knowledge that becomes available as part of the initiation experience occurs by way of connecting with the spirit world. This connection is established through dreams, visions, direct energetic connection with nature, soul journeys, and through the administration of hallucinogenics. All of which spoke to me, as I sought a death to cure me of my cancer of my culture. Little did I know the death that needed to die was of my egocentric self.

They say your initiation begins at the moment you feel there is something greater than yourself moving through you. Something beyond just who you are as a name, a member of your family, your role in community—you know it when you encounter the grounding of being and the miraculous essence of that all-encompassing truth—and you will never the same.

When you are awake and listening to the world around, you become beholden to walking a path that reflects a communion, a sense of belongingness that can only be experienced when individualism is dissolved and with it, one's sense of inflated importance. Here, all alone, stripped of all my labels, armor, and other external shields until I was naked and afraid was where I would learn the value of humility as my teacher and of the unknown, unseen world as my classroom.

Questing for a Vision

A rite of passage is an individual and community way of marking the transition between one stage of life and the next. The individual embarking on the passage does so with the intention of claiming completion of one stage and the initiation into (beginning) the next. For many people in our post-modern society, the notion of ceremony has disappeared and with it a lost sense of connection to things greater than ourselves and the story of how we are in connection to those things. Developing a conscious narrative with intentional choice to move into a transition aids us in successfully integrating change, rather than being subject to it. A rite of passage is one form that facilitates a transition with intention, structure, and support to guide us into a deeper understanding of what is happening to us. This is done through the skillful act of mirroring a person, but does not try to explain, rationalize, or justify the experience for us.

Robert Moore, American Jungian analyst and Distinguished Professor of Psychology, Psychoanalysis and Spirituality at the Chicago Theological Seminary, gives context to the importance of acknowledging the need for severance and ceremony whenever an "old psychological adaptation has outlived its usefulness and must be transcended." While others may object, fearing that such acts will invoke feelings of anxiety and loss of control, many such as those wounded warriors I sat in council with as well as myself can no longer heed the path we are on and thus set out for an initiation. While this path is clearly a transitional one for the individual, it is nonetheless essential for the health and well-being of the individual's community as well. For the whole cannot shed the structures that binds it until the one does, for they are one and the same. As author Sebastian Junger best articulates in his book *Tribe*, "Belonging to society requires sacrifice, and that sacrifice gives back way more than it costs, that sense of solidarity is at the core of what it means to be human."

One day as I was visiting a friend, I went on a walk in the woods. Hungry for renewal and desperate for initiation, I had a profound calling to do a vision quest, *right now* the voice yelled at me, *you are ready*! I stopped in my tracks and started calling the two people I knew who guided fasts. One was full, but the other had one last opening for a women's fast, which was to be held in a few weeks. I signed up immediately and went home to tell my family of my intention of doing this fast: that I was going to go out on the land, without food and shelter, to die my ego death and pray for a vision of healing and direction in my life. Suffice to say, my children were fearful I might die by going without food for four days and my husband thought I was beginning to lose my mind. Neither were wrong per se: I am going to die, but this initiation enables me to choose a psychological ego death over my physical human death. On November 10, 2015, I set out for Death Valley, California and an experience unlike anything ever before.

Up to this point, I knew little of this ancient ceremony beyond its calling for a person to engage in the sacred journey of self-in-transition. A vision quest is a healing journey that calls the initiate to leave her familiar world behind and live on her own, away from the usual distractions of everyday life, in silence and contemplation with the land. These surroundings also offer a powerful reminder that, while we are human beings, we live within another spirit, full of beauty, power, and healing of untapped potential for all. This type of journey is archetypical in many lores from our wisest ancestors to more modern-day poets and businessmen, all of whom walked away from their modern world in search of something greater for themselves.

Cultivating intentions. As a ceremonial medium, fasting is one of the oldest in the world. Fasting is like cultivating the soil of our human nature; the body is tilled and emptied so that a seed can be planted for the spirit to grow. Steven Foster and Meredith Little, pioneers in vision questing for the modern world, write that "Fasting nudges the body up against an instinctive fear of death, foreshadowing the ultimate emptiness. The initiate makes an agreement with fear saying *I will allow you to fill my emptiness—so that I and my people may live more fully.*" A vision quest is truly a journey inward. You have very few material things: a sleeping bag, emergency supplies, maybe a pen and pad of blank paper, toilet paper, tarp for under/over you, a flashlight, and maybe a change of clothes. You are venturing out for four days and nights with no food and no external stimulation of any kind to dive deep within yourself as you've never known before—or at least as far as I had ever known before.

Basecamp was held at Stovepipe Wells, California. It is hard to believe this location of one small lodge, coffee shop, campground, and corner market could be considered a town, but it was. Twelve women met in the afternoon to gather and ground ourselves as we set up our tents, walked the land, and enjoyed an evening meal together before the opening ceremony. We then spent the next four days in council hearing each other's intentions for our vision and getting ourselves prepared mentally, physically, and psychologically. On the fifth day we packed up a few things and drove to our quest location to find our individual place on the land for our four-day solo.

The pilgrimage of life itself is a process of dying and being reborn, of emptying and filling ourselves again full of purpose and meaning. The quintessential rite of passage is our birth, life, and death of this physical plane on which we currently exist. Beyond that, all rites of passages within our physical life are about aiding transitions within as a means of preparing ourselves for that final passage. In search for transformation in support of my growth towards wholeness, I am reminded that self-actualization comes through those acute moments that the psychologist Abraham Maslow called "peak experiences." Peak experiences provide a person with a rediscovery of a self beyond the ego, "as the essential Being of the world is perceived by the person, so also does the person concurrently come closer to his own Being." Rites of passages therefore exist, first and foremost, to remind us of the liminal state we are in today and of our eventual ego death to be reborn. This is what I sought to experience.

Finding my spot. They say that the place one chooses always expresses something unique about the psychic landscape of the initiate's inner being; this is one of the ways our outer world mirrors our inner world. Similarly, how one finds their quest spot says a lot about the state they are in at that time; both were most certainly true in my case. As I arrived at Lemoigne Canyon in Death Valley, my whole being was uneasy. To find my spot I initially set off in an easterly direction thinking that if I am seeking a death and rebirth, where better to be than in the East? Unfortunately, not in the East, South, West, or North could I find a location that felt comfortable to me, or more so, to my psyche. I ended up walking for hours and hours, long after my sisters had found their spots, and I still had not accomplished the simple task: where do I want to hold my ceremony? By now, the sun's shadow was beginning to loom and I was tired, broken, and frustrated. Coming to the painful awareness that my way of doing things was one of going until I was completely exhausted and then still not being good enough: the story of my life, right there, center stage for me to witness. I was so frustrated, having been on my journey and sacrificing my soul for almost two years by this point, I wondered why I couldn't get a break? I wanted to quit, run away, and I hadn't even begun.

It was now dark and time for our last meal and gathering together. I was numb, very uncomfortable, and growing nervous at the whole idea of this fast and being alone out on the land—thinking that perhaps I had gotten myself into something I was not prepared to do. We ate stone soup and gathered for one last council before the morning as an act of committing to each other our promise to stay safe and reminding ourselves of our intentions. We then laid out our sleeping bags on the ground and fell asleep under the stars.

That night I had a dream. I dreamt I was on a grassy hill looking down on docks on the water. I could see a row of boys, lined up in front of a man; between the first boy in line and this man was a hole in the dock. I then saw the man wrapping a rope around the first boy's arms and across his chest, as if to lower him into the water, under the water, and restricting him from freeing himself. I then realized that the first boy was my son, Nick. A flood of fear rushed over me as if I felt every emotion Nick was feeling as well as those of his mother: the loss of control, the potentiality of dying, and intense fear as I was screaming at the man, *what are you doing to my son?* I rushed down the hill and flew onto the dock as Nick looked at me and said *Mom, it is okay, this is my initiation, I have to do this*. I realized then, as I woke up, that this dream was about me, about my initiation, about my going under the water—water, which is the symbolic form of consciousness—for my initiation. I could not go back to sleep.

Crossing the threshold. We were awakened at 6:00 a.m. to come together around the threshold. In this gathering we stepped, one by one, into the circle to be smudged and purified and then were ceremonially handed over to the Great Spirit to become spirits ourselves. When I was ready, I stepped into the circle and said my intention: *to be open to dying the death of the old me and to welcome what I am to receive about my rebirth*. I cried a deep cry; I did not know why or where it came from. I only knew it needed to come out. When they were complete with smudging me, I stepped out of the circle, walking away from my sisters and away from my community, to venture into the unknown dark shadow of my soul.

I picked up my backpack and ventured onto the land, walking slowly and feeling my heart beat hard. As I arrived at my solo spot, I was once again not content with it and went looking for a better spot than this. *Ha!* As if I would find a spot anywhere on this land that would calm my nerves. As long as I was out there alone, without the distractions of modern conveniences, I would continue to be afraid of the slow passing of time and the deafening roar of the silence I was not used to.

I decided I would set up my tarp for sleeping. I found a nice sandy ledge that welcomed my sleeping bag and would be comfortable to lie on. Unfortunately, as it was a soft, sandy ledge, it was a hard place to set up a tarp. For the next three hours, I struggled with how to put up a tarp at an angle, in a location with no shrubs, on a ledge that was fragile, with the exception of the sharp volcanic rocks and with no knowledge of how to tie a rope or how to properly set up a tarp tent. I did everything wrong. I set it up wrong over and over. I tried to go slowly and patiently, as if I had all the time in the world. I was telling myself that this was a good way to stay busy and pass time, since time was moving excruciatingly slow. Like the day before in finding my spot, I eventually became fatigued from trying too hard.

Here again was another example of my incompetence and inability to perform a task in front of me, and adding to this agony was the pain of my bleeding hands. The rocks are porous and very unforgiving, so over time my hands began to crack and bleed as I wore them down, caught between the rocks and my ego in my fight to "get it right." I decided to take a break and to walk up a dry stream bed, toward an old wagon I had seen the day before, to meditate. The funny

Transcending the I

thing is that before coming to this quest, I imagined myself spending the entire four days sitting peacefully and meditating or doing yoga. Thinking I would be like the yogi on the mountain, in pure joy and harmony in the silence around me as I was alone on the land, my experience was anything but that.

The external world mirrors my internal world. As I sat there and meditated, trying to be grateful for the time in silence and the space around me, I started to feel the wind pick up a bit, growing ever stronger. I heard a voice in my head telling me to go back and check on the tarp. When I arrived, my tarp was flying in the wind as it hung on by a thread. I once again doubled down to secure my tarp to whatever shrub or rock I could find. The wind was growing stronger and the shadows of evening were already beginning to form around me. Nighttime comes early when you are butted up against the western side of a mountain in the middle of winter. I could feel a growing unease within me.

They say that a wilderness fast alters the civilized consciousness inside of us. Here, out on the land, the psyche is open to the orchestration of the elements and rhythms of the natural order of things as it all rushes into the pit of the stomach in an unknowing, unfamiliar, sense of wonder and awe. I sensed the winds around me setting up for a banquet, as if I were the main entrée of the feast laying at the doorstep of my master to cook within me, stir within me, all the magic of her kitchen. I was beginning to regret my intention to die. I was begging to the Great Spirit that I did not mean a real death, that I do not want to die a real death, that it just sounded good to say. Although truthfully, I knew I needed to die a death of the way I used to be, body armor and all, so that I could crack open to receiving a new way of being. But here, in the early hours of twilight, all my fears, known and unknown to my consciousness, were rising up and were loud, strong, and scaring me.

As that night fully enveloped me, I lay there alone and cold with a terrible windstorm brewing around as well as within me. All the ways in which I had set up my tarp resulted in it being woefully inadequate to survive the night intact, though what I really felt inside was that I was scared to death and unsure of my ability to survive the night intact. My flesh was pressed hard into the Earth as everything around me whipped uncontrollably in gusts so strong I could no longer hold on. It would appear that Mother Earth knew not of my ego, or perhaps she did, and she was there to remind me that I cannot ignore her as she rips my tarp away, calling to me, *you cannot hide from me* and exposing me like a vulnerable newborn—stripping me once again of all my attachments as a reminder that nothing can come between her and me no matter how hard I try. My bloody hands were a reminder that I would destroy myself if I continue to cling to and fight for my life rather than just be. That night I felt like Mother Nature was laughing at me and mocking my incompetence, and then adding to this my insecurities with an ensuring panic attack that pushed me over the edge. The fear was so deep; it was one that I had not felt in over 20 years and came raging back in a heartbeat. I grabbed my sleeping bag and a flashlight and ran back to basecamp.

Since we were in the spirit world at this time, basecamp had told us that if we came back for any reason they would ignore us as we got what we needed, unless we approached them for specific help. I told them my tarp grommets failed, that I was panicking, and that I could not do it—I was too scared and uneasy. They lovingly pointed me to the van that had brought us and told me I could sleep there that night if I wanted to. It was very cold and the wind was unforgiving. Feeling ashamed and embarrassed, I climbed into the Suburban. I was not happy with myself and chided my incompetence as my sisters weathered the storm outside. Exhausted, I fell asleep. That night I dreamed about levitating; it was now the second or third time I had this dream over the past week, and every time I started to stand up, but could not get my feet off the ground.

I awoke about 5:30 am, long before the sunrise of 7:00 a.m. I stared at the early dawn sky, relieved that daylight was coming soon. Never had I ever been so consciously aware and grateful for the rising of the sun as I was this morning. I walked back to my solo spot with my sleeping bag in hand and my head hung low. I decided to move my spot somewhere closer to the main camp so I could feel a bit more secure at night and off the ledge of sand and rock. I found a decent spot closer to basecamp on a flat surface with an ample amount of options to which I could tie my tarp.

Carving out one's ego. With the day ahead of me and nothing to do, I was bored, nauseated, and beginning to be overwhelmed by the deafening silence around me. Walking seemed to help, so I readied my daypack and set out on a journey not sure where I was going, but glad to be out and about. In Death Valley, the terrain presents a vast openness and a heightened awareness of the fragility of life. Here I felt so exposed, without purpose, misplaced on a land where it would be impossible not to see me. This reminds me of a poem about the Woodcarver (Chuang Tzu in Merton), where he writes of setting aside the time and space, away from ego, from caring, and from the ills of the real world. In that liminal place, where there is no space or time, there is also no location for who I am or where I am, let alone *if* I am. I walk about, I wander, I am betwixt and between, dead but not born, in that pregnant pause. During this time, I came to see how fatigued I was from fighting myself or fighting something out there in an attempt to gain control—not just of this vision quest, but of my life. Already, in less than two days, this vision quest had managed to mirror so much of me and how I showed up in my life: I struggle, I fight back, I work against myself, and I never slow down to breathe and enjoy life.

It was still very windy and I continued to walk aimlessly, nowhere yet everywhere my feet would take me. Slowly, my awareness started to shift as I realized it was again time for the bewitching hour of twilight, that time when the shadows start showing deeply among the rocks and land around me. What little grace I had enjoyed for a few hours was to be quickly replaced once more with fear. Once again I was uneasy, trying hard to fight back the panic. I hummed, sang, recited the Buddhist mantra out loud over and over again; all as I tried like hell to silence the suffering that was going on inside of me. I knew it was all in my mind, yet despite my intellectual knowing that I was safe, my mind said otherwise and I was unable to control its command over me. I walked as I tried to distract my fears; I deeply did not want to go back to the van, but with darkness enveloping me and the wind smacking my soul once again, I panicked and grabbed my sleeping bag to head back to basecamp. Even more humiliated and wishing like hell I was not there, I climbed inside the Suburban and wept uncontrollably.

The humility of fear. Humiliated, I kept wondering to myself, how did I get to this point? How did I come from a world where I was so strong and always in-control to my inability now to be alone on the land for even one night? I used to be the one others looked to for direction, yet there I found myself in a world where I could not even sleep outside alone, a mere 200 yards from other people. I wondered what was going on inside that had so much control over me, especially at night? Then I began to remember how at home, at night, I used to drink and watch TV or work more to distract myself from my darkness. Inside with the lights on, with the busyness of my tasks and the objects of my distraction, I hardly noticed the world outside. But out on this land I could not hide from my suffering; instead I was consumed by its darkness and felt vulnerable in its silence. Out here there were no distractions for my soul—no easy cure, pill, drink, drug, shopping, internet, or anything else to distract me from my mind. It was as if I were pulled deep within myself toward my darkest fears while simultaneously catapulted outside of myself to observe a person who is ruled by illusionary fears and anxiety, which perturb her even as they exist nowhere other than inside the cage she put herself in.

At one point during the night I thought I heard a noise so I sat up and as I reached for the door I heard the world *love* said to me loud and audible, yet it was also in my mind, inaudible to others. I knew, beyond a shadow of a doubt, that this came from the great mystery, the Great Spirit, Mother [Earth] telling me she loves me, reminding me she is there for me. I knew that this was not for the benefit of my being told that everything would be all right, but rather this was to give me an awareness of my slowing down to be able to hear her message of love. Somehow, some way, I knew I could do this, so I got out of the car, walked to my tarp, laid down and resolved to get through the rest of this night, and all the others, alone.

After surviving that night and two more following, I arrived at my last day. By this time, I was loving my time on the land, loving my conversations with the butterfly who flutters with me, the lizards who sit in the sun with me, and the jack rabbit who teaches me how to jump while running. The sacred and profane had flipped again and what I once feared I now loved. The world out there was a stark difference to the one I had been living my whole life and yet, hard as my landing was, I did not want to leave. The world *out there*, the one people call the *real world* of form, structure, rules, governance, laws, and hierarchies, seem so unreal, so false, so wrong compared to the beauty and wonder of that land. The simplicity of a slow pace is unparalleled to the frenetic stride of the modern world, and I wanted to never go back. Not that I did not want to see my family, but rather my values had changed and I no longer desired those material objects that once held me so deeply.

As I was walking on this last day of my fast, I had less energy than days before and so I would stop to rest more often. My last rest, on a comfy rock, had me staring off into the distance as I tried to take it all in when all of a sudden a raven stopped and sat on the rock right in front of me! I said "Hi" to him and asked if he had anything to say to me. He just stared at me. I then saw him doing something with his throat. I don't know what it was, but he looked like he was gagging on something when suddenly he made a noise: he was talking to me! Not the usual screeching sound, but he was actually talking. I kept asking him what was he was saying to me and, although I couldn't figure it out, I did know he was talking to me. At some point, maybe two or three minutes later, he cleared his throat with a familiar screech and flew away. After a few more minutes I got up to go back to my solo spot and, while I did not know what he said, I had this overwhelming feeling of forgiveness—not a forgiveness for anything specific—just a whole heart, whole-being forgiveness. I remember feeling so light and so full of gratitude for this moment and his gift for me.

My insignificant self. On the last night of your fast you stay up all night waiting to receive your vision. I began my evening with a death lodge. A death lodge ceremony involves remembering the people in your life, regardless of situations or circumstances. Sitting in a death lodge, relationships and the events that happened with people, their meaning, all tend to look very different than they might have at the time of encounter. The most important work of the death lodge involves bringing healing and completion to relationships. In your lodge you have the opportunity to spend time, in spirit, with people who have been significant in your life. What needs to be said to bring completion and, if needed, healing to these relationships? What needs to be forgiven, and are you willing to do so? What contribution has the other made to your life and growth that needs to be acknowledged? How can you best honor the other before you say good-bye? Your desire here is to thank and honor each person for the role they have played in your life and to say good-bye. Once this is complete, you are at peace with your life your community, and your God: ready to move into the world of spirit.

As I was sitting in my death lodge, I contemplated how the ashes of my body will someday consume about as much space as the small rock in front of me. I began to internalize how, at the end of my life, this is about all my physical body will amount to, dust and ashes, so why do I live my life for so much physical or material gain and ignore my truest essence? Out here I realized what I needed to shed; what needed to die that evening was my attachment to outcomes, to the duality I created in my life between having and not having, being good enough and not being good enough, and between life and death. I came to see again that my worse fear is not my death but is the discovery that I had never really lived when the time comes for me to die. Many indigenous traditions are said to encourage crying at a birth, for that is the beginning of death, and they celebrate at death, for that is the beginning of life. This night, as I sat alone in the darkness of my soul and more frightened than ever in my life, I kept reminding myself of this truth as I held vigilance for my vision.

After my death lodge and a few hours of sleep, I awoke around 2:00 a.m. to go into my purpose circle, another ceremony held during vision fasts on the last night. This time I faced the East, with the cross of my grave at my back, waiting for my vision and rebirth. The East is the place of spirit and new life, just as a new day begins with the sun rising every morning. The Dalai Lama says the Tibetans lost their spirituality [Buddhism] until they were kicked out of Tibet. His story goes that in the dark of night, fleeing for their lives, they found what they had lost—their purpose. He says they were cold and isolated before that event; the world knew little about them. But in their exile, they found their voice and role in the world.

Healing from Mother Nature

As the night neared its end, I had a profound awareness that I was going somewhere else, even as I never left the physical plane. I was being led into a castle-like setting and quickly shown all my psyches. As we rushed past them, we began down a circular stairwell into a poorly lit dungeon where things looked much different from being above. Dirty and cold, we rounded a corner toward a jail cell. As I approached the cell I looked inside and saw a girl around the age of eight or nine sitting in the corner disheveled, scared, hungry, and frightened. I scooped her up and told her I loved her and that she was safe now. This little girl resembled me sitting in my driveway waiting for my mom to come get me all those years earlier.

Next thing I knew, I was above ground holding this girl in my arms until she absorbed into my body and became a baby in my womb. She was inside of me and I was now pregnant, joyfully rubbing my tummy as she grew until I eventually gave birth to her. I brought her close to my chest and nursed her, told her how much I loved her and that I would always be there for her. I loved her so much and as she got older and a little farther away, I was still there loving her.

Suddenly, she was a tree. But this tree, alas this girl, was me, and the ground, my mother—Mother Earth—was telling me how much she loved me. Telling me how much she cared for me, how she has always been and will continue to always be there for me. She told me that no matter how tall I got, how far away from her I grew, that she will always be holding me close and nourishing me with her love. She told me that when I am old and can no longer hold myself up she will gently lay me down, receiving me back into the bosom of her beingness where I will join her once again. We are always connected, and she showed me how life is a sacred reciprocity—for without her I would die, without me the children would die, and without any of us she would die.

The experience of being taken into another world, a waking dream so to speak, is beyond the English vocabulary to explain, for there are no words that can serve such a phenomenon. In my vision I was guided through the rooms of my psyche and down into the dungeon that held my little girl. As I gathered her up, carried her in my womb, and nursed her into health, she became me and I became her, both held by the love and giving of our mother. It was a profound vision, which yielded so much love and healing inside of me. As I came out of this vision I realized that my vision quest journey was not so much about my rebirth but that it was about my wounded inner child, that little baby girl I had repressed and cast aside along with my dreams a few years ago. Here in my vision, I was given the gift of life back for this wounded little girl and for myself. As the sun rose I was amazed at my transformation over these four days. I now had a sense of peace as my monkey-mind was calm and relaxed, and most of all I felt more safe here in the wilderness than I ever had in the real world.

One more dream. After we headed back to basecamp, we broke our fast (break-fast), showered, journaled, and went to sleep early. This night I had a dream I will never forget. I was inside an open-air room on hard, compact dirt as many people gathered around in small groups, talking amongst themselves. Next thing I knew, I am lying down and starting to rise slightly above myself. Levitating like my last dreams, only this time I rise off completely off the ground to hover a few feet above. I could see my physical body sliding slightly down the dirt mound a few inches away from me. I looked above me and I saw the sky full of dark gray and white clouds, swirling overhead in a manner that was not inviting, though I was also not afraid of them. I then see these currents, like electricity, all around me but they are moving laterally across the Earth, not coming down from above. These electric currents are holding me from rising any higher, telling me it is not my time.

What I experienced while I was in this state is a sense of pure joy and bliss. Not the physical weight of the human world—nothing like that, I can't explain it—but what I can say is that it was beyond this world. I had no weight in this state, I carried none of the weight that this physical world demands of us. When I woke up the next morning I was so full of love, I knew I had just experienced what it was like to not be of this physical world. There is no explanation possible for what I experienced as there are no words or other expressions which can account for this. Just pure love, pure bliss, pure everything.

Coming home. While it takes enormous courage to go on a quest, it takes even more courage to return home. The journey home can be scary, alienating, and isolating. The quester has experienced something most in the modern world

Transcending the I

wouldn't understand and there are no words for the experiences felt out *there* in that other world. This was most certainly my experience. For most people, the descent inward sets the stage for our rebirth, for reincorporation, for the rejoining of the body with community and for a new beginning. The return home begins when one crosses the threshold once again, renouncing our spirit form and reentering the world of structure, rules, and governance. Birth emergence requires a loss of freedom. I utter the words of Franciscan friar Richard Rohr, reminding myself of how my false self must constantly manufacture itself; that is why it is so nervous and insecure: "The true self only needs to uncover, discover itself, it is already there."

As a quester, my return back into the "real" world happens through physical forms such as eating, showering, sleeping, and talking about the challenges of returning home. It is through food, water, community—those solid elements of nourishing and cleansing our bodies—that we remember ourselves with the waking up of our consciousness. This reentry often includes a few simple ceremonies such as the giveaway. For the gift of one's quest to be real, it must be given away to one's people; it must be made useful for the community in a concrete way. To signify the willingness to make one's vision useful, each person gives a gift to someone else in the group. This physical gift becomes a touching reminder of the precious inner spiritual gifts received during the trip.

I continued asking myself: am I a more whole human as a result of my journeys thus far? Have I changed my understanding of who I am, what I believe, and how I live? Sure, I came home from Nepal and traded my Lexus for a Leaf, but is that enough? Isn't that just an external symbol of something most people want to portray about themselves to others? I began to see that physical changes in who I am was not going to be enough. I needed to get deep into my core of who I am and what is preventing me from truly becoming who I am to be as the fullest expression of my authentic self.

Loneliness Hurts

I have been warned that the liminal state can be intoxicating and once experienced, many do not want to return from it: I know I certainly did not want to. Out here in the peace and silence, we all found ourselves wondering why we created the world we have and pondering how we can continue to escape it. Alas, the point of a vision quest is not to escape the world but to find our way back to our people to help those communities we belong to grow closer in connection to each other, and the blissful world around us, that I had just experienced.

It turns out that community and participation in one's community has a profound positive effect on our physical and mental health, longevity of life, and happiness. Research demonstrates again and again that loneliness kills and it is the quality of our relationships that matter most. A 75-year study of adult development demonstrates that good relationships keep us happier and healthier and people who are lonely live shorter, less happy lives. Having weak social ties is as harmful to health as alcoholism; in fact, a lack of social activism is as damaging as smoking fifteen cigarettes per day.

When I came home and tried to tell my story, I soon discovered I had no one to truly share my experiences with. As I would begin to share parts of my story with family and friends, they would stare at me as if contemplating whether I was going crazy or involuntarily committing me. Perhaps I had reached the edge of their comfort zone just as I had reached mine. At best, most people avoided the conversation topic entirely, which meant they avoided me and I was even more lonely. Worse yet, they would make a joke about it as if to ease the tension. I know they all meant well, but I found myself sinking deeper within loneliness and depression,

Seeking an Initiation

holding my time on the land as sacred and protecting it as if it were my truest existence.

As a result, the rebirth experience for me was a bit like dropping a newborn baby into the body of a full-grown adult with all the burdens and responsibilities of caring for this newborn self in addition to her own family, work, and other earthly commitments. Confused and bewildered, seeing the world I came from with new eyes, I did not like what I saw around me. I wanted desperately to climb back into the womb of my mother on the land. The time out there felt so much more real to me, so much warmer and full of love when I compared it to the icy, external, materialistic world I created around me. Just a few days earlier my inner child, my little girl psyche, had emerged to be nestled and fed by her mother's love—where was she now, I wondered?

To some degree, a setback should be expected; after all, one needs to be continuously tested in order to keep the vision burning. Rather, it is the fading away of the feeling of connection, of the sacred energy and purpose that was felt while alone in the desert that I missed the most. My sense of freedom and connection was so strong, yet as I returned back to the "real" world, doubt crept into my thoughts as if to question if what I experienced *out there* was real. For the vision to grow, I know I must hold it deep within me as a

Transcending the I

sacred seed being fertilized until it is ready to fully blossom, but being home for several weeks, praying and crying for my people to come forward, for a *knowing* of who I belong to and what gifts I can bring them, I sink deeper and deeper into despair, loneliness, alienation, and depression. I was grasping for any wisp of a hope that crosses my path, all of which hold no knot at the end to keep me from slipping off again and again. I had never felt a depth of loneliness such as this.

Chapter 6: Fear Kills

The best way to deduce the system's purpose is to watch for a while to see how the system behaves. – Donella Meadows

In his book *Soulcraft,* author and wilderness guide Bill Plotkin writes of how "contemporary society has lost touch with soul and the path to psychological and spiritual maturity, or true adulthood. Instead, we are encouraged to create lives of predictable security, false normality, material comfort, bland entertainment, and the illusion of eternal youth." Moreover, we have lost our connection to nature and the oneness of the universe, instead filling our days with distractions in an attempt to muffle the cry of our souls in the name of fear. Fear of death, fear of the unknown, fear of the silence, and fear of having to listen to our souls cry for us to be different and not knowing where or how to begin. Often these distractions become our addictions: consumerism, eating disorders, substance abuse, pornography, workaholism, religious fundamentalism, obsessive thrill-seeking, or gambling and excessive TV watching, all of which contribute further to the deterioration of the world. In these expressions of our being we can see how our fear is expressed in the form of these restless activities.

Our fear has to be acknowledged and faced. We need to find the courage to look at how we move, how we talk, and how we interact with others, all of which demonstrate our fear and discomfort with being alive today. It is time we realize our fear and reconcile ourselves with the meaning of our impending death and, more so, face the realization that many of us are living a meaningless life full of value that is defined by our economy, not our hearts. As the Dalai Lama writes, "True fearlessness is not the reduction of fear; but going beyond fear. When we are afraid we cannot handle the demands of the world and then our fear expresses itself as a feeling of inadequacy".

The severance of my self started with disassembling who I was through the death of my value system and living by external definition. As the sacred and the profane have flipped in my life, I round the corner of my transformation into a place of trust and vulnerability, to further discover who I truly am to become. The next path of my journey called me to venture into the world, not on a pilgrimage or in ceremony, but rather to witness and experience the harshness of a world consumed with fear, greed, and not enough love.

Peace and Security

One day, out of the blue, I found myself reading about an international conflict prevention, resolution, and reconciliation symposium in Bologna, Italy. I knew nothing of the International Peace and Security Institute (IPSI) or of peace and conflict in general, but I had a deep calling to participate. I was sure this symposium would be discussing the role of governments, regimes, opposition, and power as it all pertains to conflict and violence, but I wondered, do they discuss the role multinational corporations have in influencing governments and their policies? I felt to hold this symposium without this as part of the conversation, they would be missing a critical component of the discussion, so while I had no idea what I was doing, I filled out the forms and answered their questions.

Why attend symposium? The first question asked of me was why do I want to attend the symposium? Rhetorically, I responded, asking them to please help me understand how, in a world where 51 percent of the dominant economic forces today are corporations versus 49 percent countries, can the leader of a large corporation today not be responsible for the economic, social, and emotional balance and equanimity in the world along with all other world leaders? I can't imagine that pressure: do you choose profit and market share for your shareholders or preservation and dignity for those who don't hold your future in their hand, though perhaps you may hold theirs? It is a morally unbalanced and unfairly loaded question at best and I wondered how we can help leaders work through this challenge without sacrificing our people or planet with questions such as:

- How do they build a human system where the value is on the whole person showing up and doing their purposeful work, not just living as a cog in the wheel for a paycheck and title?
- How do they empower everyone within to make the best decisions based on the lived values of the community and not get corrupted in espoused values and self-worth?
- How do they produce the best products possible for shareholders and customers as well as for all the lives impacted by the manufacturing and disposal of their products? And,
- How do they use their organization as an agent of change, where profit and power are not the dominating measures, but are instead in balance with the concerns of people and planet?

I felt strongly that rather than laying the problem and solutions at the feet of governments and their political leaders, oppositional forces, and NGOs, what about corporations and their growing involvement in our world's economic, political, and social dimensions?

The next question they asked me was *what does being a peace and security leader mean to me?* I wrote of a Native Americans story about a sacred tree of peace. The story goes like this: Once upon a time as the nations of this world were at war with each other, the leaders of each nation decided to come together to *bury the hatchet*, so to speak. They gathered up all the arms [weapons] within each of their nations, came together, and under a large tree dug a hole to throw all the arms into so there could be peace upon the world. The prophecy is, a day will come once again whereby the leaders of all nations will be at war and come looking for this armory to destroy mankind. They say that the only way to end the prophecy is if all the children of the world come together, gather their [human] arms around the tree, and protect the tree with love and connection from those who want to destroy. I told them this story because it represents, for me, a metaphor for what it means to be a peace and security leader. My role is to help bring awareness to our destructive patterns of behaviors, highlighting the bright spots, and generating hope for the future we desire to create, while at the same time supporting a path for future generations to seek the tree, to seek peace, and to continue advancing what I hope we are able to begin.

It turns out that, as a result of my deeper inquiry, they changed elements of the symposium to consider the inclusion and results of corporations in our political discussions, and thus accepted me into their five-week program in Bologna, Italy where I sought two main outcomes:

1. To gain the skills and insights about how the private sector, in particular multi-national corporation leaders, may play a more active role in promoting peace and easing conflict in society.
2. To learn more skills and taxonomy related to peace keeping, conflict management, and mediation/ negotiation processes related to conflict.

Slowing down to connect. The first day of the symposium we did a get-to-know-you exercise. We were paired up in groups of six or seven people and sent out on a scavenger hunt to discover Bologna as we got to know each other better. Our team decided to pare down even further, into groups of three, each assigned half of the questions in an attempt to divide and conquer. I was paired with two other women: one from Syria and the other from Pakistan.

The three of us set off on our journey. In typical fashion, I set us off on the task of accomplishing as much as we could, as fast as we could, with winning as the goal. I was walking fast so as to not lose any time, hurrying us amongst the other people in the center square towards what we believed to be the first location, which housed the answer to a question. At some point, I turned around to ask my two partners if they were getting thirsty and realized they were far behind me. I stepped back to observe our difference in attire: while I was dressed in outdoor shorts and tennis shoes, they had flat sandals and were wearing a modern, yet still traditional, Jilbab, a Muslim long dress and head (but not face) cover. They were not dressed for any aggressive form of walking nor were they accustomed to walking in such a fashion. This made me reflect deeply on what was automatic pilot for me: to be aggressive in my pursuit of winning without realizing the needs of those around me. I reminded myself that the purpose of the game was about getting to know one another, not about winning. This lesson was not just the lesson of this game, it was a lesson I am to learn about life. Pursue at all costs is not a badge of honor or courage, but rather one of ignorance and ego. I was grateful to be able to acknowledge this rather than be frustrated because of a false conditioning of my mind that they were slowing me down toward a goal, as the old me would have irritatingly thought.

As the heat rose with the day, I was growing thirsty and offered to get us some water. It was at this point I was reminded of one other important difference between us: our faith. It was the month of Ramadan for them, of spiritual cleaning and renewal. Chapter 2, verse 185, of the Quran states:

> *The month of Ramadan is that in which was revealed the Quran; a guidance for mankind, and clear proofs of the guidance, and the criterion (of right and wrong). And whosoever of you is present, let him fast the month, and whosoever of you is sick or on a journey, a number of other days. Allah desires for you ease; He desires not hardship for you; and that you should complete the period, and that you should magnify Allah for having guided you, and that perhaps you may be thankful.* – Abdel Haleem

What this means is that on this hot July day in Italy, these two women, in addition to not being dressed for the task, were also going without food and water from sunrise until after midnight, for an entire month. Sebastian Junger in his book *Tribe* asked the question, "How do you become a man in a world that doesn't require courage?" to which I would extend: how do you become a whole human in a life that asks of no sacrifice? Humbled, I took a deep breath and knew my lesson was to slow down and connect, to learn more about them, and use this game as the instigator of our encounter, not the motivation of my intention. I did not want to mirror the fast-paced, "no pain, no gain" Western axiom they already feared. Disassembled, I wanted to avoid any possible re-assembly of my being, which included the familiar pattern of frenzy and urgency towards a goal over the slow pace and connection with others along the way.

One view, two realities. Over the next few hours we walked many miles in the hot sun and during this time I asked many questions about their world. At one point, the Syrian woman looked at us and commented on how nice it was to talk freely, with no fear of someone overhearing you at the cost of punishment or worse, death. She lingered in the beauty and peace of our surroundings and sounds; those same surroundings and sounds I found ugly (graffiti on walls) and annoying (loud car noises). She paused in the silence of no bombing, no gunfire, no fear of what—or whom—might be looming around the next corner. I reflected upon her words

Transcending the I

as deep within me stirred a greater awareness of how different our lives were. Of how I go about my daily life complaining about traffic, cold coffee, and too many emails. My *first-world problems* seemed petty and self-absorbed when compared to theirs.

We continued walking and discovering Bologna for a few more hours when, at one point toward the end of the day, we came upon a two-story multi-business building that held the answer to our final clue. I told the other women I would go to the top floor and they could walk on the cool grass below to relax. As I was walking along, I came across two men who were listening to music, which I took to be Islamic prayers. These men helped me find a particular business and when we were done, I pointed out my two friends below and how proud I was of them and their fortitude for following the Islamic tradition of Ramadan. At that point one of the men looked at me, as if in disgust, and said "Oh, they're Muslim" as he drew out the last word repugnantly. I thought to myself "Oh shit, they're Hindu," knowing that Hindus and Muslims have a somewhat tumultuous relationship in some parts of the world. My worry was not of my safety, but of my new friends. I have never before had to worry about the repercussions of what I say in public or of my religious beliefs, but I was not in America and they were both from somewhat conflict-torn countries. I hurried down the stairs and quickly moved us all back toward our dormitory, confessing my story along the way. While this impacted them little, it had a deep impact on me. It is one thing to read about religious oppression but quite another to experience it firsthand. Albert Einstein once said, "Peace cannot be kept by force; it can only be achieved by understanding." I believe this understanding cannot be learned through books, YouTube videos, or other media, but rather must be felt inside, witnessed by our body as the representation of a judgment against a deeply held belief. What I experienced on this day was the beauty of diversity we each have within us, met with the harsh reality of the fear of our differences, and how this fear can shrivel and silence the beauty we share.

Over the course of the next five weeks, I got to know 39 people from 28 different countries, with the majority of those being Middle Eastern, Eastern European, and Northern African. Every person was kind, open, curious, and eager to learn from everyone else. All but three of us were under the age of 35, the majority being mid to late twenties—basically a twenty-year difference between us three old folks and the rest of the participants. This was a new experience for me, to be the oldest person in a room and to feel the generational gap between us. Occasionally, I was reminded of which age group

I came from when the youngsters felt frustrated about the state of the world and wanted to blame my generation, as well as my country. They were angry at our greed and sole focus on domination and consumption at all costs and for our lack of care and compassion to help solve greater social challenges such as poverty and malnutrition among those who suffered as a result of our privilege. I can say they were wrong to feel this way, yet it was a powerful learning experience for me to witness a sense of hopelessness in the younger generations at the state of the world today as a result of my culture's attitudes and behaviors. Their perspective of being from a different part of the world, holding different values, and being a different generation, aided in my expanding awareness into the fragility of those social bonds, which either tie us or divide us.

Peace is not the absence of conflict. At this symposium, I learned how leaders seek to divide communities, nations, and the world as a means of achieving power over a large group of people. One strong and recent example of how this works is apartheid, which was the systematic institutionalization of racial segregation and discrimination in South Africa whereby the white minority sought power over others—in this case, the Black South Africans—and did so by dividing them and limiting their movement without permission. While this deeply discriminatory practice supposedly was abolished in 1991, the practice is still routinely used by leaders all over the world, albeit in less obvious ways. I learned that the United States spends more on pet care than on peace-building, more on plastic surgery than on educating our children, and more on military weapons of war than on just about anything else in the world. Little did I know that in the world of military prowess, America is the king of all arms dealers. We may not take war head-on, but we foster, support, and aid the proxy wars to ensure we remain in control and the almighty most powerful; yet, control what and powerful over whom?

Most of all, I saw how conflict begins when we each hold onto our ideologies—those beliefs, roles, values of our culture—and become unwilling to look at another's point of view. Misperceptions with no basis or desire to understand is ignorant and harmful. I believe that until we each challenge those beliefs we hold onto, conflict will remain and we will continue to misunderstand the other.

What essentially drove me to attend the peace and conflict symposium in Bologna was my desire to acknowledge how our polarized political climate does not allow for sincere discussion and as a result, we do not have sufficient tools that encourage people to meet one another on common ground. In a world where we barely have the time to slow down and be aware of our own behaviors and beliefs, where or how can we find hope to come together as a collective whole? What I was not prepared for was the reality check I received with regard to where I came from and how obliviously I had been living in my Western bubble. There in Bologna I watched videos of young African men forced into militias and trained to rape and kill others. I watched them brag about raping and brutalizing women as if they existed only to serve their sexual needs, and I cried for days at the horror of what I witnessed, vowing that I had to change something, if only myself. No longer could I sit back home silent, ignorant, assuming that what is happening in other parts of the world had nothing to do with me. I understand better now my naïve ignorance in being unable to see how the other person and myself are one and the same.

Susan

In addition to all I learned, I also experienced this rage first-hand through the befriending of a woman my age whom I'll call Susan. Susan had retired a few weeks earlier after 25 years of service in the United States Air Force. She and I had rooms at the end of the hallway across from each other and, since most everyone else around us were about 20 years younger, we quickly got to know each other. My first experience of her was that of a rather defensive, rough-exterior woman who was used to having to protect herself physically as well as emotionally. She walked and held herself with a wide stance and solid footing, as if to be prepared to either receive or give an order at a moment's notice.

As I got to know Susan, I quickly began to see patterns of a fast mind, similar to the one I held a few years earlier, always trying to think as far ahead as possible as a method to out-maneuver the enemy. She mirrored me in many ways and so I had the chance to see the impact of a person whose mind races so far forward during a conversation, as if to identify ahead of time what the other person *really* wants, so as to stop any form of attack before it can happen. I used to do this; I would try to figure out someone's angle or how I could leverage their position and then moderate my behavior based on that, rather than listening and being open to what the other person had to say first.

Creating our reality through false beliefs. Susan believed that people from many other nations, in particular the Middle Eastern or Muslim nations, were anti-American. She absolutely believed this to be "so obviously true" based on her personal experiences in the military. If someone from one of those countries stood up to say something that remotely resembled putting down the United States, she would attack

Transcending the I

them in an attempt to "shoot them down" before they could finish their sentence. At first it perplexed many people; then it angered them. Her behavior created the reality she believed. Her experiences of the world she lived in created a reality whereby she was convinced all the other people at this conference knew nothing and instead were "ignorant kids who just want to blame us while they happily take our billions of dollars and resources to aid them." A few times she found occasion to outright yell at people and accuse them of their false beliefs and then run out of the auditorium in a heated stream of cuss words. The more she behaved this way over the course of the month, the more these people began to judge the United States, and its people, by her actions. I was bewildered and did not know what to do.

On the weekends, Susan and I would try to get away and explore other parts of Italy. It was such a paradoxical experience for me because I felt a warm, caring, loving, wonderful person crying to come out in her, yet I experienced her so immersed in external armor to protect her soul that any contact rendered me harmed. It reminded me of the armor I used to wear when I sat in the corporate boardroom being distant and judgmental. Susan brought me to tears many times, not because what she said was wrong or even hurtful in intention, but because the delivery of her message was so harsh and cruel. It was yet another paradox where she was right, but her delivery was spiteful. She thought she was doing me a favor being so matter of fact, but it was hard to understand the learning in the moment as I was fighting back the tears, usually unsuccessfully, which would then yield another lecture from her that my tears were not her fault. Nonetheless, I stayed with her as an act of love and took the learnings for the gift they were.

On reflection, the learnings and experiences I received over this month were necessary for me for two main reasons. First was that I needed to witness the pain of the world, I had to hear the pain and suffering that is going on around the world at the hands of human beings, and I had to understand the conditions from which conflict escalates to violence. I saw and heard from the persecutors in the system (men raping women and children) and the victims (women, children, young soldiers) to get a more internalized understanding of how much we all suffer as a result of violence and war. The second reason was to personally witness the impact of this violence and pain by experiencing how much pain Susan was in, how isolated and conflicted inside she was, and how her pain leaches onto others, which causes more pain and suffering. I had to physically feel some of this pain, in a subjective, experiential way and not from the sidelines, not from the corporate boardroom, or not from objectively reading a book.

I came to recognize how I was living; oblivious to my role in others' suffering by ignorantly living as a *have* while the worlds *have nots* were silently suffering far away. Through awareness and contemplation, I understand now that to bring our world together, we need the response of non-anxious leaders who are capable of calm, steady, quiet courage—one that requires the skill of listening without judgment, naming without denial, and exploring issues without predetermined solutions in mind. I saw how the more intractable our differences appear to be, the greater the need to create space for something unexpected to emerge. Most of all I internalized how, in the silence and emptiness of contemplative stillness, an opening of possibilities within myself, as well as for others, can spring forth.

Letting go. I was leaving the symposium at the end of the month for my pilgrimage on the Camino de Santiago with my friend Marjorie. Susan had agreed to take my luggage and laptop back to the States for me and I would arrange to get it from her when I returned. On the morning I was at the airport flying to Spain, Susan decided that I had abandoned her and was very selfish for doing so; thus she was very angry at me and ordered me to come back to her or she would refuse to help. I was now faced with missing my flight and possibly my pilgrimage or losing all my belongings.

As I sat at the airport in tears, hurt that she would do this to me and frustrated at this whole month and how broken I was as a result of all the violence and destruction I witnessed, coupled with my violent and destructive relationship with Susan, I decided the only thing I could do was to let go of it all. That the greatest gift I could give myself was to still love Susan in that moment and to let go of all my attachment to everything I owned—my favorite clothes, shoes, makeup, books, and my laptop full of many photos and memories, various artifacts I had created, and more. It was another one of those divine moments where it hurt so much, but by leaning into it further I was able to release it all. Though I can't say it was easy.

Letting go. The theme of letting go is a primary one in my story on many levels and is best illustrated through an old story about two monks:

One day, two monks set out for a temple in a valley beyond the woods. While cutting a pathway through the woods, they came across a choppy stream they needed to cross. There, standing by the bank of the stream, was a beautiful young maiden dressed in silk. She was clearly at a loss as to how to cross without getting muddy and wet.

Without thinking twice, the elder monk gestured that he would pick her up. Shocked, she obliged. He put her over his shoulder and waded across to the other side. The younger monk, dismayed and uneasy at what he had witnessed, followed.

Upon reaching the other side of the bank, the elder monk put the maiden down gently. The maiden paid her respects and walked on. The monks then continued on their way to the temple. As they navigated through the forest, the younger monk, still troubled by what he'd seen, asked, *"How could you do that? We aren't even supposed to make eye contact with women, let alone pick them up and carry them!"*

Without a thought, the elder monk turned to the younger monk and said, *"Brother, I set her down on the other side of the river hours ago. Why are you still carrying her?"* And with that, the elder monk turned and continued leading the way through the forest, leaving the younger monk to contemplate his words for the remainder of the journey.

The moral of this story is that the compassion of the elder monk to put the needs of the maiden before his own spiritual practice, and his mental ability to then let go of the fact that he had strayed from the path of his personal commitment without feeling guilty or disappointed, is a lesson for us all. The letting go of our past is necessary to move forward today and learn we must also accept the transient nature of life; that Mother Nature will demand us to adapt and change as and when she sees fit. This will involve personal sacrifice for the greater good, as it did for the elder monk in this story. To resist this transience will only bring about mental suffering and anguish in our lives.

Chapter 7: My Greatest Challenge

Not until we are lost do we begin to understand ourselves.
– Henry David Thoreau

We find today that the once dense fabric of relationship-based social economies that value long-term sharing and cooperation has come unraveled. Corporations have emerged as the dominant governance institutions on the planet, with the largest among them reaching in to virtually every country of the world and exceeding most governments in size and power. Our political system is increasingly run by money, not votes, and it is the corporate interest rather than the human interest that defines the policy agendas of states and the international bodies. All the while, corporate interests are taking over human interests, our attention is diverted, hijacked by the electronic information and media messaging that distracts us from the things that matter most to us. In these distraction, our responses are dulled and we receive news in such an overwhelming amount of sound bites that we can barely grasp reality from what is on the screen in front of us. We drown in bits of information that engulf our self-awareness and dilute our connection to the real world around us. Not only is our attention hijacked, but our imagination is as well, diminishing our capacity to envision what we might yet create.

In the book *Walking Sacred Path*, Lauren Artress writes of how our hope needs to lie in our finding the strength and courage to change, "to be pilgrims walking on a path, we need to participate in the dance between silence and image, ear and eye, inner and outer. We need to change our seeking to discovery, our drifting into pilgrimage." After my month in Bologna, I needed to find the courage to change even more; I needed to walk.

Pilgrimaging the Camino de Santiago

The Camino de Santiago, the Way of St. James, is a sacred Christian pilgrimage walked by hundreds of thousands every year. Gratefully I chose the Primitivo route, which is known as the original or native *way* and is much less traveled than the Camino Frances. That said, it is much less traveled because it is much hillier and harder than the others. Although for me, this solitude and the incredible rugged beauty served to be just what I needed—a good butt-kicking from Mother Nature herself. Victor Turner saw parallels between pilgrims' experience of pilgrimaging and the concept of communitas, specifically existential communitas, which is characterized by the "transient nature and direct, immediate, and total confrontation of human identities." Turner explored pilgrimage, such as I did, as creating a type of liminality. A pilgrimage is a transition rite that bridges a geographic distance and symbolic distance between the profane and the sacred.

Lost and in pain. The first morning we woke up, took our time getting ready, and began our pilgrimage around 9:00 a.m. As we looked around, we realized that the familiar Camino shell symbol, which is our guidance system, does not have a specific arrow to illustrate direction. We did not know which part of the shell meant which way we should walk! This was hilarious, as the most fundamental thing we needed to know, which way to go, we never thought about until this point, when no one was around. We made a choice and began walking, eventually finding some others pilgrims who showed us the way forward. We should have been more prepared, to be sure, but I learned a valuable lesson in communication and dependency on others this day… and many more to come.

About 12 kilometers into our 35-kilometer first day, I was already in a lot of pain because my backpack was far too heavy. I was not prepared mentally or physically for this challenge and I was in tears once again. At first, it was the violence and hurt and now it was the physical pain and attachment to those things that hold me back. After 10 hours

Transcending the I

of walking, it was now late, dark, and the only albergue (a Spanish hostel) within miles was full. You apparently need to arrive by 3:00 p.m. to ensure a bed, but there was nowhere else to go and we could not move. Gratefully they took pity on us and said they would put two twin mattresses on the floor in the kitchen for us to sleep on after everyone else went to bed.

As we sat there on a hard bench, starving, watching others make warm food, have fun while eating, and clean up all while we waited, I was beside myself. I eventually mustered up enough energy to shower, but I felt old and ill prepared. I washed some of my clothes, hung them outside, finally made some rice and then eventually made my way to the mattresses. By this time two more pilgrims had arrived and so there we were, five strangers all sleeping together on two twin mattresses on the floor of another stranger's kitchen in a foreign land. We did not care, we were tired and grateful for a place to rest our weary heads so we squeezed together and slept. I remember thinking, if this is day one, can I last another 15 days? Little did I know at that time that over the next few weeks, each and every day would ask, demand of me, even, to offload something I was attached to.

Morning came far too soon. I was tired, exhausted, and my everything hurt. I went outside to retrieve my clothes and realized they were gone. I had lost my only flannel shirt, a pair of pants, and socks. Not sure what happened to them, I was disappointed but also too fatigued to care beyond the realization that I now owned just one pair of pants. Eventually we set out again for another long, grueling, and exhausting day. We quickly learned that we needed to be walking by six or seven in the morning and even then, we were two of the last people to arrive at the albergues every day. The walks were tough and I had to muster up so much internal fortitude day after day until it started getting a bit easier. What got me through those early days were the albergues at nights. I met so many amazing people from all over the world who were gracious and opened their hearts, minds, and homes to serve us.

To walk the Camino as a pilgrimage is to offer oneself a brief respite from the hustle and bustle of everyday life, it is a time of introspective and a chance to pay attention to the small things that get forgotten in our busy lives such as the beauty in the day, how the wind blows, or the song of a bird. When I arose in the morning, I would get up and put my feet on the Earth, breathe deeply, and observe myself, my environment, and the people around me. Over this month, I walked with people from all around the world, some who were walking for days and others who were spending months or even years on a pilgrimage for their life. For me, when I met people while walking the Camino, I had the time to truly hear their stories, connect with them as fellow pilgrims who accepted each other as we are, no expectations otherwise. Passing one another over the course of days and weeks, I learned to watch out for them and even care for them when they developed a blister or worse—even if I did not know their names or speak their language. Out here I got a taste of what it is like to worry about things I normally don't in everyday life; such as wondering where my next meal was going to come from, will the next albergue have a bed for me to sleep in, or will I have to walk seven more kilometers when I can't walk another step.

Awakening to within. They say the Camino gives you what you need and I joke that I apparently needed my butt kicked. I say that truthfully, for not only was this experience the hardest physical request I have ever put upon my body day after day for 15 consecutive days, it was also the hardest mentally. The fortitude I had to pull up from within to get through this was, for some reason, harder than anything I had ever experienced before. The more I walked, the more I realized what I have been seeking these past several years was not "out there" for me to find or experience, but rather it was always "right here," inside of me. My pilgrimage was not about my external experiences but rather the internal—and I struggled every step of every day.

On my pilgrimage, I realized that for me to continue searching externally for what is already within me, within all of us, only serves to continue my suffering and attachment to my ego mind. I realized that for me, awakening is not some enlightenment I am going to find out there that will enable me to lead a blissful life forever after. Awakening is my journey toward interconnectedness, it is my awareness of being one and yet nothing simultaneously. That my deepest awakening will come not from grasping or searching for something out there, pilgrimaging if you will, but merely from just letting go of what I hold on to most in here, inside myself.

Zombie apocalypse. When it came time for me to fly home, I had never been so homesick in my life. So much so that I traveled home a few days early, desperate to see my family and longing to spend the rest of the summer with them. I arrived in London with 75 minutes until my connection to Seattle, enough time, I thought, to go through customs and claim my bag, find the check-in counter for my connection, and get to the gate for my flight. By the time I had arrived at the counter, there were 40 minutes remaining until the flight departed; however, no one was at the counter and no one

Transcending the I

came after several minutes continued to pass. I searched high and low for someone until they informed me that they close the counter an hour before flight for international departures and thus, I could not get on this flight. I was tired, hungry, and homesick, and the family was having a neighborhood gathering that I desperately wanted to attend. But alas, not only did I miss my flight, they made me pay for another one. No offer of apology, discount, or other, just a cold matter-of-fact business persona and another 24 hours before I could go home. I was crushed, crying, lost and beside myself. Disappointed, I surrendered to this reality and searched for a hotel inside the airport.

By now I was very hungry so I made my way downstairs to the airport grocery store; but nothing could have prepared me for what I was to experience next. I got off the elevators and at first it was the smell that overwhelmed me, perfume and cologne everywhere, as if every person had doused their entire body with a bottle of something. Next it was the bright lights all around as masses of people all mindlessly shopped for products they did not need. But the most disturbing of all was when I looked into people's eyes and they were hollow, empty, as if on autopilot in a desperate search for something outside of themselves to satiate the overwhelming stimulus. Making this more frightening were the soldiers with big guns ordering the people into single-file lines and no one seemed to even notice or care.

What I witnessed this day was a world where humans felt empty of life. This was not something I witnessed with my rational mind, but rather my heart and soul were sincerely afraid that this is what humanity was now reduced to. My heart wept for the world I experienced there in the airport, as I found no space for silence, contemplation, or connection with one another. Void of the natural world I had just been immersed in, this world felt plastic, cold, and distant as I had never experienced before. I could not grasp what I was experiencing. I had been away from normal social life for almost two months and this return was far more than I could bear. Inside the grocery store, I grabbed a few bites to eat as fast as I could and ran upstairs to my room, locked the door, and wept for humanity. How could we have become this way, I wondered, and why would we submit to such a way of living every day? I was devastated by the whole day and quickly fell asleep until the next morning and my return home.

Wounded soldiers. As part of my journey learning about war and conflict, I came home and sought to learn for myself, as much as possible, what it is like for our brothers and sisters to go to, and then return home from, war and conflict-torn areas of this world. I have never known much about this part of our reality before and so I wanted to hear for myself what struggles they have re-incorporating into society from their lives as soldiers. I befriended a veteran in Olympia, Washington, and would occasionally go visit him, help out in his community garden, and spend time in council with other veterans, sharing our stories. Jokingly, I told him how I had always considered myself a *wounded soldier* for the war I came from, but through my experiences with him and other veterans in council, they reminded me of the war, and that wounding within, I had created for myself. Worse yet, one could argue that their war is a result of my behavior and desire for *more* at all costs, though they never said that.

In council with veterans, I heard stories of pain and struggle, of how the system is failing to support even their most basic needs, and of how 22 veterans commit suicide every day. My friend himself spent six months with a needle in his arm and a gun at his head while his children ran around wondering what happened to their father, but no one else sees this because they hide it inside the four walls of home. I witnessed this pain as I heard his stories about the fights with his ex-wife and as I witnessed his daughter lashing out as a young teenaged girl, drinking too much, running away with the wrong people, and worse of all, trying to commit suicide more than once. I know we have the economic and psychological resources to aid their desperation, so why does society collectively choose to turn away from those men and women who risk their lives to serve our safety?

Human behavior and fear of social stigma reduces us to ignoring, or worse yet, not recognizing and hearing the wounded stories from our soldiers. Our indigenous cultures knew that when one man goes to war, all go. Therefore, it was the responsibility of the community to welcome warriors home, to bring them back to witness their stories, and then to provide them with a role in the community where they provided meaning and value as a human. I sat in council with these men and women, hearing the horror stories of what they went through to protect the rights I enjoy every day…ignorant of the lives that fall so I may continue to drive myself and this world into the ground with my fear-obsessed, overworked sense of self. We all fail our soldiers when we don't allow them to tell their stories and instead push them aside to remain alone in the dark so we don't have to witness their pain. For my act of behavioral change, I aided this man through tough times; most notable was that I dragged him off the couch, paid for him to spend a month in the mountains learning the way of wilderness guiding, and then supported him as he began one of the first veteran-only vision fasts in this nation for our wounded warriors who feel called. I am proud of supporting this soldier in finding purpose and meaning in his life and I pray he is able to spread his passion to other fellow soldiers in aiding their healing, growth, and transformation as well.

Home. Emotionally spent from my two months abroad, I was grateful to be home with my family as I curiously wondered what lay ahead next for me. My Camino pilgrimage partner, Marjorie, belonged to a Buckminster Fuller visionary leadership team and had begged me to go to a *Bucky's game* event in Southern California for a day. I was reluctant to go, as I had just returned home, but since she flew to Italy to trek the Camino with me, I thought this was the least I could do for her.

On an early Saturday morning in late August, drenched from head to toe from boarding the plane outside in a driving torrential downpour, I flew to Southern California to participate in a Bucky's game event. This global game was interesting in many ways, most notably that in this game you model, through action and play, the way the world is structured. The modeling included each person portraying the population and political climate of each continent. So, for those of us on the continent of Africa, as I was, we were very poor and there were many of us crowded on the playing field. For lunch, while Japan and the United States ate a large buffet with lots of leftovers, which they threw away, we each received a cup of rice and beans with a quarter cup of water. Furthermore, when we tried to rise up and break away from our oppressive governments by leaning on the United Nations or World Bank, we came to see how they often make a situation much worse, as they are controlled by global powers who are not interested in giving up their power to help others. I was exhausted, as this day mirrored much of what I had experienced in Italy and the reality of my world smacked me in the face yet again.

Iowa

The next morning, as I was getting ready to catch a cab to the airport to go back home, I met Colin* (name changed). Colin was a man who was passionate about water—and money. He had started a bottled water company many years ago and brought it to a reasonable level of success before selling it to his partner because they could not get along. Colin was now starting a new business in partnership with a wealthy businessman named Tony* (name changed). Tony had been in the commercial real estate/shopping mall business for several decades and built his company to be worth a few billion dollars by the time he retired. Tony and Colin recently had struck a deal with a local foundation and some Wall Street bankers to be the sole proprietors of a new technology for drilling water. Their espoused hopes and dreams were to bring this new water to communities all across the United States, along with bottling plants, enabling local economies to have access to unlimited water, plastic-free bottles, and neighborhood food hubs focused on community health and well-being. Additionally, they wanted to provide the ability to tap wells for farmers, Native Americans on dry reservations, and others who might not have easy access to fresh water. It seemed a dream too good to be true.

This company was registered as a for-benefit ("B") corporation and the proceeds of that corporation were going to a non-profit, for which they wanted me to be the president. This non-profit would focus on building community hubs in every town across America to improve the health and well-being of all Americans one village at a time. To begin this new initiative, I spent the entire month of October, 2015, in Iowa, learning and experiencing first-hand about our nation's food quality and water supply… or lack thereof. To my horror, I learned what industrial agriculture means for the average American, how our nation's local farmers have been marginalized to the brink of poverty, the devastation and inhumanity of confined animal feeding operations (CAFO), and how our government is lining the pockets of large multinational corporations at the expense of individual and communal health and well-being. All the while we throw away excess food, nearly a third of our total supply, as a quarter of America's children go to bed hungry every night.

Industrial death. I remember sitting in a town hall meeting in Fairfield, Iowa. I had spent the day at the Maharishi school of consciousness (Maharishi created *transcendental meditation*), seeing how the kids meditate before and after school every day, how they learn to grow their own food, then cook and eat the food they have grown, and how they share the bounty of their harvest with their community— in addition to meditating, of course! That night in the Fairfield town hall, I heard the stories of farmers who are literally dying because of the CAFO's upwind of their farm and family homes. I heard from farmers who desperately want to do the right thing, to bring fresh, organic, wholesome food to the marketplace for you and me, while earning a decent living from their efforts. Sadly, what I witnessed was how the system has them marginalized and fighting for their right to farm at all. These farmers gave example after example of how Monsanto steals their crops through poison and power, how large agriculture companies want to own all the farms, and how the marketplace calls *organic* a *special* supply chain just so they can mark the prices exorbitantly high, despite the fact that none of this increased money gets back to a majority of the farmers.

That night I learned that CAFO hogs live their whole life in the space equivalent to that of a yoga mat, if they are lucky. They have no room to turn around, lie down, or roll in the mud, for there is no mud, only slats for their waste to fall through onto the ground and into stream waters below, which then flow into the city's water supply for the citizens of Iowa to drink. These hogs are fed a diet of antibiotics, antifungal and pesticide-laden food grown from genetically modified seeds; they never see the light of day until they march from the barn to the slaughterhouse. Even then, approximately 10 percent die on the spot from the stress of seeing the sun for the first time. I can't help but wonder what all the stress and sadness of their lives, not to mention their cocktail of drugs, does to our bodies when we ingest this meat?

I researched how the percentage of *food-insecure* people in the United States is greater today than during the 1960s, about 15% now compared with 5% in the late 1960s, and more than 20% of U.S. children today live in food-insecure households. Furthermore, the industrial food system is linked to a new kind of food insecurity: unhealthy foods that lack the essential nutrition to support healthy lifestyles. We are confronted with a growing epidemic of obesity and related diseases, such as diabetes, high blood pressure, heart disease, and a variety of diet-related cancers. There is growing evidence that America's diet-related health problems are not limited to poor consumer food choices or processed junk foods, but they actually begin on our dinner tables with a lack of nutrient density in food crops produced on these industrial farms.

Organic but not safe. To experience this even more, I went to the home of a scientist Colin knew who had invented a sensor chip that could test for the pesticide Boscalid, an antifungal pesticide to reduce or eliminate soil-borne white mold in our food. Little is known about this carcinogen's impact on our bodies, as we save those tests for the rats and mice. Regardless, we opened a plastic bag of organic lettuce leaves and took one leaf to test for Boscalid presence. The United States Food and Drug Administration (USFDA) limits this toxic substance in our food to 6 parts per million (ppm) or less as organic, between six and thirty ppm as safe for human consumption, and over thirty ppm as toxic to humans. As he tested one leaf, it came out to 5.2 ppm, hence qualifying as organic. He then educated us that while the USFDA limits lettuce to 6 ppm per leaf, or less, as organic, the measure of acceptance does not take into consideration volume or amount of substance reasonable to ingest.

Meaning, while one leaf is organic, two leaves are not, for the exposure is additive. Two leaves would be 12.4 ppm, safe for humans but no longer organic. By the time you get to 6 leaves ingested, you are at exposure levels exceeding 30 ppm. A typical salad contains many lettuce leaves and thus, he exclaimed, you may be safer to eat the plastic bag than all its contents. I was floored.

Life had taken me to Iowa, once again, to witness the oppression and marginalization of minority communities when pitted against corporate America's pursuit of market-share and growth. In 2016, sustainability researcher, John Ikerd wrote, "Whenever and wherever family farms have been replaced with CAFO's, 90% or more of the independent family livestock and poultry producers have been driven out of business because corporate agribusinesses use contractual arrangements to manipulate markets in ways that prevent independent farmers of even having access to competitive markets."

I was angry and disgusted at our system. Furious that more people are not aware of this, or perhaps they do but the implicit agreement in society today is that if you don't tell me the consequence of my purchasing habits, I'll ignorantly keep complying. By my fifth week of traveling to and from Seattle to Iowa, I found myself coming ungrounded, crying with the

My Greatest Challenge

lack of balance in my life and growing frustrated with this supposedly dream job. I found Colin to be a very likeable person, but he was demanding and unreasonable in his actions towards me. I felt he did not know what he wanted from me, yet he expected me to know what to do. Colin had no time to slow down, no time to strategize, no time to help bring others along. He was myopically focused on raising money and how we can claim market share; he cared about little else. His actions mirrored all the behaviors I was seeking to lose.

I sat in my room the night of week five, once again distraught and missing my family, and I had a profound insight. Colin did not own a home, he rented a room; he did not own a car, he rented his car monthly; he had no wife or kids, no dog, and no responsibilities. Colin woke up every morning and went to work; work was his life as he had no responsibilities outside of work. After work he went to the local restaurant or pub for dinner and drinks—lots of them. When he would pick me up from the airport or when we would drive across the state, he would drink and drive, text and talk on the phone. When I asked him to please not do this, he would say, "This beer has practically no alcohol in it, it doesn't affect me" and continue on. Adding to this was the occasional chauvinist joke, calling me "honey," and other sexual advances—all of which helped push me over the edge. I felt so disrespected.

Life continues to mirror aspects myself. Bologna, Camino, and now Iowa—life had taken me to its outer limits to witness the oppression and marginalization of so many communities when pitted against corporate America's pursuit of market-share and growth. In reflection, what I came to be aware of was how Colin's behavior essentially mirrored who I was when I worked for ego, stature, and the pursuit of more at all costs just a few years earlier. How he resembled me through his work, which defined him and was the reason for his existence second only to his need to drink at night to numb himself from the way he lived: alienated, isolated, and alone. I flew home that Thursday evening and was supposed to fly back on Sunday. On Friday, I emailed Colin and graciously backed out of participating in this company; it was not for me. I had realized that this journey represented a few things for me. First it was the perfect combination of my old way of being (working endless hours, ignoring responsibility of daily life, drinking at night) met with my dream of working with a leader to bring about change and transformation for global good. He also was a prime example to test my need for patriarchal approval, which had been the basis of my life starting with my desperate need for love and attention of my father. This opportunity, and Colin, came at a time I was desperate for some way to define myself through work aligned to my new value system, but that was the problem. While the project may have had the right words to denote a change of priorities and altruistic values, my ego and the method of achieving this job was entrenched in the familiar patterns of social separation, individual power, and market-share goals rather than passion with a purpose. As another behavioral act of my change, I walked away.

Depression

After the year of being exposed to world problems of violence and power, then walking a pilgrimage for healing and strength, to discover how these world problems play out in my own nation, I found myself spiraling deeper into confusion as to where I was going and what was I to do next. I thought Iowa was to create the "perfect" job for me, but instead I found another empty promise built on an empty pursuit of greed and market-share over passion and purpose. I kept trying remind myself that this was a time in my life of going inward and letting emerge whatever might emerge, but that is tough when we were struggling to pay the bills and I was feeling insecure in all the ambiguity around me. Adding to my increasing confusion was my husband's growing dissatisfaction with his work, or more so with his management team, and this was starting to reflect at home. I empathized with the position I had put him in, as I know he wants to support me as well as provide for our family, but he was beginning to feel trapped and neither of us knew what to do. I was growing desperate not to cave in just yet and re-enter the corporate world —I was not ready and there was still more of me that I needed to experience.

Drowning in my suffering. My depression was deep in my gut, as if the loss of a loved one had just occurred. I felt lost and did not know where to turn, who to turn to, or what to do to help myself. As Sebastian Junger wrote, "A person living in a modern city or a suburb can, for the first time in history, go through an entire day—or an entire life—mostly encountering complete strangers. They can be surrounded by others and yet feel deeply, dangerously alone." This was how I felt. No one around me could understand why I would want to go out on the land alone, why I would want to fast for four days, or why I would resolve to sleeping on the ground amidst the storm around me. Perhaps they did not understand the greater storm deep within me? How do I explain how the deafening silence of the land helped calm my nerves, how the wisdom in the conversations with a raven and a butterfly gave me the forgiveness I needed, or how feeling Mother Earth's chest beating against my fragile beingness strengthened my resolve?

As my marriage was challenged between this and other financial pressures from my not working, I dug deeper into schoolwork and prayed more fervently for something to save me from myself. I continued drinking wine, as I wanted to drown this hurt deep within me and pretend it was all a bad dream. By this point I had gone from experiencing the frenetic busyness of corporate life to seeing the majestic mountains in Nepal and their reduced snowpack, the fragility of life in the dried-up lands of Botswana, the poverty and destruction of war imposed upon four-fifths of the world by the privileged one-fifth, and the chemically laden industrialized farms in America that poison the very communities they are meant to serve. Each experience was laced with greed, competition, and consumption as the basis for all the suffering and destruction within its environment. But what do I do and where do I go from here? In my not knowing, I continued to suffer and drown my sorrows in the agony and shame of what I created and experienced.

In late January of 2016, I got in my car and started driving south to California. First to San Francisco for a week of school residency, then to Esalen for a week of an inaugural Wisdom Women's conference, and finally to Ojai for a week of council training and even more time out on the land. Council is a practice of open, heartfelt expression and attentive, empathic listening. Participating in a council meeting teaches us how to let go of personal expectations and become fully attentive to others. In this gathering of speaking and listening fully from one's heart, wisdom flows in the stories told as well as the silence in between. Passing the talking piece with the intention of speaking authentically and listening attentively inspires deeper communication, intercultural understanding and the non-violent resolution of conflict. The four guiding principles for council are:

1. **Speak from the heart**. Speaking from the heart is about telling our personal story in a movement towards vulnerability and authenticity as the whole story is weaved.
2. **Listen from the heart**. Listening from the heart is a practice of staying centered on what is true for us rather than what our mind thinks or how our emotions react.
3. **Be lean of expression**. An invitation to speak what is in the present moment without fill or backstory.
4. **Garnish spontaneity** – Resist what the mind is thinking about saying and feel for what story is deeper inside trying to get out.

My Greatest Challenge

The council circle is like a momentary threshold, a place of temporal transcendence into a different way of being in relationship with self and others. A severance from the "doing" state of existence, offering a gathering ritual to allow for a greater story of the whole to emerge. The circle offers a moment to remember that we are not alone but rather that we are inexplicitly interconnected, as if by magic, when our stories all weave a common theme.

On the morning I began my drive home, I received a call from a local nuclear energy design company that was looking for a consultant to help them assess the state of their organization's culture, strategy, and information management systems, all in an attempt to turn from startup to a mature organization. Excited and anxious, I drove straight home as fast as I could. *Finally*, I thought, *could this be it...my dream job of working with leaders to bring about change and healing to our world?*

Alternative energy or Band-aid to same problem? EarthSupply* (name changed) is an energy innovation technology company with some wealthy founders backing their initiatives. The heart of EarthSupply lies in its ability to bring innovative alternative technology solutions to the world's largest global challenges: clean energy and access to proper nutrition and healthcare to increase the health and well-being of all beings on this planet. It is a huge challenge that many people are

Transcending the I

passionate about, myself included. I thought for sure this was the dream job I had been imagining. It was similar to my role with Colin and water: working with world leaders to help bring about change for greater health and well-being of all, just closer to home and better pay. I was eager to begin.

For this effort, my role was loosely defined as the responsibility for looking at the larger picture of how the organization works collaboratively and how information flows, what are the people, processes, and tools that are disconnected, and how can they turn around a start-up innovation organization into a maturely functioning corporation inside a highly-regulated industry as they set out to build their first plant with, and inside of, China. As you can imagine, these tasks alone were fraught with challenges. First, the nuclear industry is the most regulated industry in the world. Second, the United States and China have several challenges in working together and collaborating on such intellectual property. Last, but not least, they are two countries who are worlds apart economically, physically, socially, and intellectually. EarthSupply work flow is highly dependent on face-to-face communications and collaboration; whereas, China is secular, competitive in a way we can't imagine, and there is a 15-hour, 5000-mile cultural gap, which is wider than the distance is long. This was the perfect challenge for me!

Not quite ready. I loved this work, I was born for this work, and I knew right away many of the challenges of this organization. The leaders feared risk, they lacked clear decision making, they had no infrastructure for communication, and all notion of progress was aligned to the organizational chart and not value created from workflow. Furthermore, the innovation leader and the engineering leader conflicted and thus held information from each other, which limited collaboration between the two most critical teams. Every bit, byte, and word had to be meticulously captured in a fragmented integration of process with productivity, as the whole sub-optimized for the parts with project management as *the* authority over human capacity. They even signed off on a 10-year project plan that was so inadequate, the engineers laughed at the absurdity of it. That said, the people were amazing and everyone held deep passion for the work they were doing. None of the challenges of the organization were a result of its people's lack of commitment or ability to get along: quite the opposite, things went very well through sheer force of the human spirit.

When I shared my findings with the leaders they were less than pleased. In the end they wanted me to tell them how to build an information systems infrastructure and give them the game plan for such a task. I had done this to some extent, but I reminded them that two other people had already done work similar to this—written many pages for an integrated management system—which they had ignored for the past few years only now to hire me, a third person, to do the same. Their issue was not in knowing what to do, it was in their fear in taking action and possibly being wrong. Like many other leaders I have experienced before, they would rather slow down and ensure permission for failure than take the risk to lead.

These leaders knew want they wanted: someone who would tell them what they wanted to hear, not what they needed to hear. I handed in my report after eight weeks and walked away. Not only because they weren't ready for me, but because I realized I was not ready for them either. I needed more time, more patience, more compassion, and I needed to finish the work I had begun. I knew I was nearing the end of my journey, but what I did not know was that I had one more year to integrate all I had experienced into who I was becoming before I would be ready for an assignment such as this and even more.

Chapter 8: Ayahuasca Teaches Me Love

Where there is love there is life. – Mahatma Gandhi

As noted in Chapter 1, after 20 plus years in a large, very successful corporation, having also achieved three master's degrees along the way, I found myself high in the organizational chart and earning a healthy income, but unfulfilled in life's purpose. Worse yet, despite earning more than $200,000 a year, I still essentially lived paycheck to paycheck and had little to show for all my hard work beyond material possessions and the pile of waste I left behind in my disposable tracks. After a gradual perturbation of my soul, I left this world and began research aimed at looking directly within myself, at the stories I told myself, which were mutually reinforced through the social culture I lived in. Digging in even further, I then researched how I would transform myself beyond the I-it, subject-object relationship I held with the world around me—and as a mirror of the larger social and cultural challenges of my world. In this inquiry I sought to answer the following question:

How can the experiences of contemplative silence, mindful awareness, and indigenous ceremony facilitate transformational learning in support of human growth toward wholeness and interdependence?

To further my personal pilgrimage and Ph.D. studies, I began asking deeper questions: how would I be able to explain, or more so demonstrate, such a transformation, through inquiries such as:

- What shifted my awareness from concern of how I wanted others to see me toward how I actually see myself?
- How have indigenous ways and nature-based connections facilitated my growth and development toward a more whole-human (physical, psychological, spiritual, or communal) lifestyle?
- Have I demonstrated transformational learning in ways others can observe and learn from, such as:
  - psychological (changes in understanding of the self)
  - convictional (revision of belief systems)
  - and behavioral (changes in lifestyle)

From these questions, and the basis of this book's stories, my journey emerged.

My Death and Resurrection

What I have come to understand is how stories such as mine are rarely just about the one person such as myself; rather they are illustrations of an archetype that rings throughout all humanity. Like the hero in Joseph Campbell's monomyth journey, this archetype is defined as a pattern, situation, character, or symbol that recurs in the human psyche at all times. The damsel in distress, the hero with a fatal flaw, the creature in the night, and more. Myths have laid the foundation for the archetypes we have come to expect in every story. But stories do much more than tell us where we are from; they also guide us in what values we hold, how we should spend our days, what activities should be our priorities, and how we should care for each other.

Stories and myths are often used in indigenous societies as a teaching tool, for those people know that the health and well-being of a whole human is a mirror of the community and vice versa, for there is no separation between the two. Yet the modern human has failed to hear the deeper narrative of life as a profoundly cooperative experience where all living beings exist only in their relationship with other living beings.

I realize now that in all ways, as we all move through our lives, we seek out those stories that provide meaning and shared experiences from which we can learn. People do not want information; we are up to our eyeballs in too much information. What we want is faith in our humanity through meaningful stories that inspire us and give us hope and belief. From great indigenous teachings, such as the medicine wheel or four directions, we learn that life is not linear, it is cyclical and that we go around the wheel many times an hour, a day, a year, and a lifetime as a way of making meaning and expressing ourselves. Stories are circular in nature themselves as well, which is how they differ from a discussion. There is no discourse on why something happened the way it did; stories transcend the literal interpretation of text. The reason for this is that there are always stories within the stories, inside and between, and finding your way through them is as hard as finding your way home when you are lost. Part of finding is getting lost, and when you are lost you start to open up and listen.

What my vision taught me is that my story is one of death, the death of my way of being in this world. Though death in-and-of itself would have been easy, this story is about my pilgrimage through the dark shadows of my soul to be reborn. This story is how trial and tribulation of one person mirrors survival and redemption for the whole human race.

During the five days on my last vision quest, nature mirrored who I was: lost in egocentric self-regard. My journey enabled me to begin seeing how I was lost in the accumulation of more, in fear of not being enough. I began to see deeply how I was living life defined through external labels of what others "out there" thought of me rather than what I thought of myself in my heart.

Why did I embark on this journey? First, I will start with what I came to realize about myself through a reflection of my generation. While my research has demonstrated that a majority of contemporary Americans have similar experiences of our modern world and its social dis-ease within, this view is not an absolute statement for all.

In my mirroring of my world, I have come to see that what is needed for our modern world to survive, if not thrive, is to change our perspective of our self and how we show up in relation to others. Rather than continuing to invest in greater methods, models, and measures to determine the reasons for our behavior and hence seek technical solutions "out there" to resolve conflict, I believe we each need to go within and challenge the underlying belief structures and patterns we hold onto. Not in search of right or wrong, but rather to seek a greater learning and understanding as to who we are individually, which will help us understand the collective much better. In my journey, I came to see how my belief patterns held me in a state of fear and constant movement as I sought validation and acceptance from others by living up to their standards of good, else I ran away.

Unfortunately slowing down is hard; contemplation, mindfulness, and time in ceremony might just be the hardest thing to cultivate in humans from the modern world. It takes time to respond intentionally and not just react to what is immediately before us. When we react, what often gets lost and goes unaddressed are life's bigger questions: How are we dealing with our grief, fear, and insecurity in ourselves as we transition individually through our lives or collectively through those cultural challenges? Are we open to not being rejected in the face of courage or do we shut down and run away, as I did all those years?

When our attempts at discussing challenging issues get coded in fear and aggressive language, it is often very difficult to pause, reflect, and then act from a stance of openness, yet we know that when we sit in contemplation with ourselves, we begin to soften the voice in our head, as I experienced early on with yoga, meditation, and Buddhism. And when we sit in contemplation together, we become more spacious in our hearts for the other as well as for ourselves, just as I experienced in Nepal, Iowa, and in the communitas of ceremony. This way of being is different from a mental discussion of a topic in a linear exchange of facts; rather it is a way of cultivating an exchange of talking and listening *with* (not to) one another with honesty and respect.

The type of transformation I modeled in my dissertation is about a way of being, not about doing, for I believe that the essence of life is less about what we have done and more about who we are. Yet modern society has led us to build our identities based on what we have rather than who we are, and thus we are left lost and confused. Organizational systems consultant and author Margaret Wheatley stated that effective leadership requires deep immersion into the pain in the world in which we live, yet doing so can require a person such as myself to experience grief, sadness, and loneliness among so many other emotions in ways that many of us would rather choose to avoid.

Ayahuasca Births a New Me

In October 2017, as I was preparing to return to the states from Germany for a "leading as a sacred practice" gathering, I received a calling—not a phone call or email—but a "knowing," which comes from deep in your soul. It clearly told me I was ready for ayahuasca now and that it was time for me to receive its medicine and healing. Not knowing where or how to find such a ceremony, I reached out to a friend who is connected in this community to see if there might be a ceremony anytime while I am in the states. At first he said no, the only ceremony remaining this year had just passed, so I sat with the intention, not knowing how to bring this to fruition. A few days later, he wrote me back and said they had decided to hold one more before the end of the year. *This is it,* I thought; that is how intentions work.

Knowing that ayahuasca is not approved for use in the states, or many other countries, I will refrain from mentioning locations, people, or any other identifying facts. I would only add that those who classify this as an illegal drug have clearly never taken it before. This is not a hallucinatory drug for pleasure and it has been proven that there is no getting addicted to this medicine. Gabor Maté, world renowned doctor and author of an insightful book about addiction called *In the Realm of the Hungry Ghost* writes of how ayahuasca is not a drug in the Western sense, something you take to get rid of something. Rather, that when properly used, it opens parts of yourself to which you normally have no access. The parts of the brain that hold emotional memories come together with those parts that modulate insight and awareness, so you see past experiences in a new way.

I began my trip to the states out on the land, sleeping amongst the coyotes and owls at night and the turkey vultures and deer during the day. Here I came to realize that my learning edge at this point in my journey is to step fully into my greatness, that authentic self of who I am, without being defined by it! While life is a perpetual experience of shedding what no longer serves, and I was thrilled at this insight. I decided to mark my transition by creating a necklace of prayer ties, 7 for each of the 4 directions, to give thanks and gratitude to the spirits while I ceremonially walked a labyrinth as a mirror of my journey the past few years. The twists and turns, going forward and then suddenly shifting, lost and exploring, all those metaphors felt right to use as a cumulative reflection. Entering the labyrinth's center, I placed my prayer ties in the circle and again expressed my gratitude. On the walk out, I unwound and released anything I still held onto from this journey to enable me to exit as a form of giving birth to what was next. It was beautiful and very healing to honor and thank the unseen world unseen for all the love and support, be it butt-kicking's and all, along the way. That night I danced joyfully for the powerful week on the land as I prepared to head out for my ayahuasca ceremony.

Mother Ayahuasca. I arrived at the gathering destination and got settled in by 6:00 p.m. Realizing I was starving as I hadn't eaten since 11:00 a.m., I went in search of food only to be informed that it was too late for me to eat as the ceremony was to begin in two hours. Come 8:00 p.m., about 30 of us, including three medicine healers and three helpers, gathered on our mats in a circle against the wall. As the medicine healers packed their pipes, they gave us an idea of how the ceremony works, what we were to expect in the physical plane, and reminded us to always ask for help when we needed it—whether that be guiding us to the restroom, emptying our vomit bucket, or just someone to hold our hands. The ceremony then began, with each of us receiving smudging and then being invited to come up front to drink, one by one until we had all received, and then the lights went out. After a few whisper-like sounds from the medicine men, we sat in dark silence for about 30-45 minutes waiting for the medicine to kick in. The medicine healers then began chanting and drumming in a variety of languages from Navajo and Cherokee, Spanish, Quechua and more. But the most bone chilling tribal singing I have ever experienced was Shipibo—the ancient tribal medicine language of the indigenous Peruvian rainforest peoples. Those chants were rhythmic in a non-linear and unnerving way that made my teeth and jaw ache because the vibrations resonated so deep within my bones.

This first night I, as the medicine introduced herself to me, I started to see a world beyond empty space: one where lines, geometric shapes, and Mayan spirit images dwell in a colorful dance of energy and flow all around me. The colors were mostly red and green, some blue and yellow. When I would see a person moving across the room, I would see an ancient Incan spirit that was protecting them or that was them, I do not know. I have read that the Shipibo sacred songs correspond to specific tones and nonlinear states of consciousness to enable the opening of states of highly organized nonlinear feedback complexity in both neural and cellular signaling pathways. By employing these techniques, the shaman can entrain the biological function of the patient all the way down to the cellular level, perhaps even to the genetic level. Either way, I was overwhelmed and my body became dead weight. I was unable to move, and a low backache that began a few days previous is increasing inside of me all the way from my legs to my shoulders. Even when I breathe I can feel a soreness inside me that aches. The songs light up every cell in my body and go on nonstop all night long, often with multiple songs at a time as they simultaneously perform "energetic surgery" on one person, yet we all received its healing powers. I have read about people with powers beyond the physical plane, but tonight I witness medicine healers whose powers are far beyond anything I could ever imagine.

This first night, I came to understand, was a night of mother ayahuasca introducing herself to me through these vibrations, shapes, and colors. I introduced myself to her through my willingness to allow her energy to flow through every cell of my being down into the depths of my soul. They say that subjects under the influence of medicine such as ayahuasca report feelings of being cleansed from the inside, like each cell is being polished and organized, and that waste and cellular debris are being expelled. This was certainly my experience on that very long, exhausting first night: emotionally, mentally, physically, and spiritually. When the night eventually came to an end, around 3:00 a.m., I barely made it upstairs for a bite of banana and then went to my room and violently threw up. Unable to move much, I collapsed for sleep.

Late the next morning, I crawled out of bed for breakfast, unsure if I could do another night of such life consuming magnitude. I did not need visions or insights to realize this work is not about those things, but rather is about the medicine and its healing powers. I rested the entire day, trying to determine if I could withstand another night.

Night two came as we gathered once again in the room, drank our medicine, and sat on our mats in the dark waiting for the medicine to sink in. Eventually the chants and drumming began and while I could feel mild effects of ayahuasca, it was not the same as the night before and even waned in effect after a few songs. Each night, after about five songs, the medicine men would offer more ayahuasca for anyone who felt called to receive a second serving. On my second night I thought about taking a second offering as I watched the woman next to me get up and join others for more. I did want more, but I was afraid to consume more because the prior night had been so overwhelming for me. I started telling myself that perhaps ayahuasca was going to go easy on me this night since the prior night had been so challenging. As I lay there, I felt the intense pain in my back and was so weak I was shaking and moaning to myself. Just then, I saw monkeys, primates, staring at me as I was wearing (or inside of) a large white wolf skin. This wolf animal has visited me before in dreams, but I had been unclear about what it meant. Tonight however I was she, though I do not know what that meant, either. I understand that for many the white wolf symbolizes wisdom to keep life in both the spiritual and physical realms in balance. The white wolf, also known as the phantom, is an important symbol of someone who lives in both the spiritual and physical worlds and helps people understand the underlying reason things happen. But why she showed up this night I need to reflect on more. I sensed, however, another initiation.

As the chanting, singing, and drumming all resumed, I could see the woman next to me now moving fully into some sort of ceremony. Mother ayahuasca then began teaching me the difference between fully jumping in to participate in life with everything one has versus sitting safely on the sidelines, waiting for something to happen—as I had just done by being too scared to take more medicine. This was not an intellectual conversation I was having; it was a full-body experience of life mirroring me and teaching me in a non-judgmental way. I came to watch the woman next to me as the representation of someone who is all-in as I lay on the sidelines observing her ceremony and wishing I was more into mine.

About this time, the medicine woman came over to me and motioned me to put my head at the end of my mat and lie on my back so she could work on me. Energetically, she put her hands on my head and heart and was working to get me out of my head and into my heart (as I was later told). At one point while she was working over my heart, I felt this intense, sharp pain flow through my chest with a flash of green light. In that moment the ceremony came rushing in as I realized she had unblocked some stuck energy which ayahuasca and she were working on.

Laying on my back, paralyzed with ayahuasca flowing through my veins, I could see my friend now crying and wailing in sorrow. I sensed that while she was fully in her ceremony, we were all connected and in that energetic connection we all collectively share, she was carrying some of the pain and sorrow I was not willing to carry. Mother ayahuasca was showing me how, when I do not address my pains and wounds, I project onto others both, literally and metaphysically, my pain and fears. I asked mother ayahuasca to please give me back any of my pains and sorrows that she might be carrying. I do not want her (or anyone else) to suffer as a result of my inability to carry my load. All of a sudden, in the flash of a second, I raised up and over my bed in an urgent sense of action as I violently threw up in my bucket several times. In that very same moment my neighbor who had been sobbing stopped crying, let out a big sigh, and laid down. It was profound to witness our connection and as I lay there empty, prostrating myself, I offered my vomit as an submission of my willingness to do this work to heal, whatever that meant. Little did I know that every night would ask of me more than I had ever given before.

As I lay there, feeling the coolness of the tiled floor against my fatigued body, I had a sense that this pit in my stomach—that same pit I fed with wine or other distractions to keep from feeling my anxiety and fears—was mocking me, telling me *"Haha, I am still here, you cannot get me out."* Exhausted with nothing more to give, I no longer cared. In my weak state, I spent the remainder of the night in deep conversation with Mother Earth. Thanking her profusely for her love and apologizing for my actions, our collective actions, and how we are hurting her, I told her I would love to help ease her pain, but I knew it was far greater than anything I could ever imagine and I feared even feeling a part of it. Though she reminded me that we all feel her collective pain, for her pain and our pain is one in the same. We all carry the weight of our actions, good or otherwise, in every one of our souls. This reminded me of environmental activist and author Joanna Macy's words when she wrote:

> *To be conscious in our world today is to be aware of the vast suffering and unprecedented peril. It is the distress we feel on behalf of the larger whole of which we are a part. It is the pain of the world itself, experienced in each of us. No one is exempt from that pain any more than one could exist alone and self-sufficient in empty space. We are not closed off from*

the world, but integral components of it, like cells in a larger body. When that body is traumatized, we sense that trauma, too. Whether we pay attention to it or not. That pain is the price of consciousness in a threatened and suffering world.

I then found myself crawling into my own mother's grave, holding her black bones and rotting corpse, and I apologized for my behavior and thanked her for all her love in my life and for being my mother. The night finally came to an end and once again I crawled into bed.

The next day I was beyond exhausted. I slept in until breakfast at 10:00 a.m., ate, and then went back to bed, sleeping until dinner at 3:30 p.m. I ate again and went back to bed, lying there until ceremony began at 8:00 p.m. I did not know if I could do this anymore; the experience has already been so intense and exhausting and there are still two nights remaining.

The third night began, like the others, with the drinking the medicine and sitting in the dark. As the chants began, I felt some effects but not a lot, just as the night before. I knew I needed to take more ayahuasca, if only as an act of demonstrating my commitment to full participation, so I went up for a second glass. I wanted to be all-in, never again would I sit on the sideline of life, fearing what would happen

Transcending the I

to me if I jumped in, for I had felt the results of my inaction from the prior night. As I lay there for a few songs, waiting for the medicine to kick in some more, a helper came to get me for "surgery" (energetic surgery) with the main medicine healer. I do not know how to explain it, but his chanting is in the deepest, most tribal tones, which make every cell, nerve, and bone in my body pulsate to his chant. It resonates so deep in me that I can feel the ancestors reawakening through my bones. He respectfully ask if he can place one hand on my heart and the other on my belly, and I consent. As he begins to chant, starting with protection for himself, I feel his hands on my body like a razor-hot knife with so thin a blade that it (energetically) cuts my skin without pain. As his vibrations change I feel different parts of my soul burn as the energetic surgery is like a heat-seeking missile to my wounds. I keep reminding myself to just breathe, that this medicine is given in full love for my healing.

I've read that this type of shamanism employs wave-based entrainment techniques to bring about spontaneous nonlinear organization of metabolic pathways and cellular signaling systems to get the patient into a targeted state (hypnosis or trance), so the shaman can then synchronize with the patient's subtle body rhythms. By destabilizing the patient's homeostasis, the shaman then uses other specialized entrainment waves to coax new metabolic interference patterns and signaling pathways throughout the patient's entire cellular matrix to bring about regeneration and healing. Whatever is going on, after about 15-20 minutes the healer is done with my surgery and, unable to move on my own, I am helped back to my mat. Shaking, paralyzed, and struggling to take it all in, I call for help, for someone to come hold my hand as I cannot move and need to feel the warmth and life of another human.

After a while and as the chanting and drumming, singing, all speed up, I tried sitting up and leaning into the medicine. I then noticed that feeling again in the pit of my stomach calling to me, but I now recognized it as my fear. I decided that instead of pushing it away or viewing it as a part of me I did not like, I want to love it and lean into how this feeling is as much a part of me and who I am as any other aspect is. The name Maya came to me at that moment and I started calling this feeling Maya. Telling Maya how much I love her, that she is me and that I would love to meet her if she was ready, but if not that I had patience and would wait as long as it took for her and I to meet. At that very moment, with intense force from a depth of my being that was beyond this physical body, a mass came up and out of me that felt like a foreign entity, and looked like an alien blob or foreign being that was deep in me. I told Maya how much I loved her and was so happy to see her, thanking her for this gift as I prostrated once again.

Next thing I know, I heard a voice talking. It was mine. I had passed out and was lying face-down on the floor talking to ayahuasca. Lying on the floor, I came to see the world from the very lowest point I could get to and was now asking ayahuasca to show me my strength and help me get up. Saying in a quiet whisper, *"Ayahuasca, show me my strength, ayahuasca show me my strength"* over and over again, she helped me understand that this is what surrender is. What I learned this night is that I cannot ask or proclaim "I surrender" with my mental mind, though that is a good start, but rather I experienced true surrender as being a state of *being* completely emptied: void of action or volition. For years I have been surrendering to whatever will help me heal, searching the entire world seen and unseen to be emptied of this self which no longer serves. Here on this night, passed out on the floor, I came to experience complete and total surrender.

Searching for strength to get up, I felt the slime on my body as I realized ayahuasca had just guided my birth onto the floor. I began to prop myself up as I kept asking ayahuasca to show me my strength until I eventually could sit. Here I began to ask ayahuasca to teach me how to breathe, not regular breathing, but learning to take every breath of my life as a breath of love, reverence, and gratitude for life. Sitting there, Maya would try to show me different things or feed me stories for my mental mind, yet I now only see Maya as love, telling her I see her and love her as all these different aspects of myself. No longer would I wallow in those stories, no longer would I give into fear or push it aside; now I see it all as one aspect of myself and I love each and every part of me. I had no more fear in my gut and my back pains were completely gone. At times when I would feel weak again, I would sit down and repeat the conversations with ayahuasca to show me my strength and teach me how to breathe with love, reverence and gratitude.

As this continued for a while and I breathed in a new way, I saw the word "masculine" and sensed I needed masculine energy. Sitting up, I called the male helper over and asked him to please sit with me and hold my hands. As I sat there holding his hands, the word "beloved" came to me and I realized that this fear was my masculine energy that keeps showing up in my relationships and in my life. I feared my masculine side and in my fear, I either pushed it away or let it overcome me in an aggressive pursuit of life. In this moment with Maya and my beloved, I came to see how I hurt others in my life when I do not embrace all elements of myself. This is not about men, per se, but is about wholeness and healing within myself, of my feminine and masculine sides. I have been living my life believing that masculine is aggression, dominance, and control, but in this moment I came to see how true love, the full capacity to care and to love myself and others, can only be when I allow the masculine energy within me to be a force of love and not fear. At this moment, in my mind, I had a wedding with my beloved masculine self, asking him to marry me and be a whole, healthy part of my being from this day forward. Putting my hand on this healer's heart, I began to ask my beloved self to teach me how to love, teach me how to live my life fully committed to love, and teach me to live in reverence to love every day.

At this point the ceremony was over, but I still could not move. I was raw like a newborn and shaking a great deal. Feeling fragile and weak, I eventually got some help to walk upstairs, as I needed a change of scenery. At the top of the stairs I stopped to sit on the nearest chair, asking for some chamomile tea, which I drank as if it were my mother's breast milk, nourishing me and healing me as mother's milk does to provide strength and nourishment. I wanted to go outside, despite the bone-chilling temperatures and two feet of snow, to see the natural world and feel her, thank her for all her wisdom, beauty, and love. I played in the snow, stared into the silence, saw the majesty in the trees. The moon was full and it peeked out from behind the clouds to light up my world. I was looking at Mother Nature as if for the first time, as the most beautiful being in the world. As winter is the North direction of the medicine wheel, I thanked the ancestors for guiding me, for their wisdom, and for their courage to walk in this world as they did.

Hungry, I went back inside to eat. At the table I seized a homemade granola bar and broke off a tiny morsel; that is all I had strength for. Bringing this crumb to my mouth, I began a ceremony with Christ as he offered it to me in a way that I have never experienced before. Despite the people around me eating and talking, in this moment I had a very intimate communion with Christ in the bread I ate and the water I drank. It was profound and beautiful. I sat there staring with the eyes of a child out into the forest and valley below, taking it all in as if life were new to me. Every breath, every step, every taste was done with love, reverence, and courage. I was born anew.

Night 4 came all too soon. Bittersweet to be ending after tonight: I was weak, hungry, and very light-headed. I was also full (of ceremony) and unsure how or if I could take any more. Feeling my mind-body wanting to run away, I tried desperately to calm it down and remain present. Drinking the

Transcending the I

medicine for one last time, I settled down for what healing might come tonight. Soon after the chants began, the third medicine man came to my mat for energy surgery. I sat up, trying to remain present to receive his medicine: breathing, calling ayahuasca to teach me how to love, show me my strength, and more. After this surgery and a few more chants, I realized how raw I was as well as very light-headed. I needed space and it felt like mother ayahuasca was calling me to the back room to see nature, yet still be close to the ceremony, so I summoned for help. Lying on the couch and weaving in and out of consciousness, I quickly realized tonight was to be a different kind of ceremony.

Rather than healing, so to speak, this was going to be a teaching night, as I had originally asked for mother ayahuasca to teach me how to love; that I wanted to see and feel her love. In that moment, she told me I was not ready to learn how to love yet because I first needed to learn how to receive love. She began showing me how all the wounds of our world are because we have collectively lost or forgotten how to truly receive love. I began to feel in my body how overwhelming love is and I saw how, when we are unable to receive love because it feels unfamiliar and scary, we instead push it away and reject it, even fear it. I began to understand a world whereby it is easier to give in to fear than it is to give in to love. That the hardest thing in the world for us humans to do is to receive love; instead we push it away and then act out in violence at our anger, which is really our wounding and deep cry for love.

I spent the night on that couch again and again overwhelmed as I was steeped in a profound realization by how immense love is. In my weak and faint state, I asked the ancestors to please feed me with the salt of their bones, to please teach me how to be nourished and fed in a new way with their wisdom and teachings. I thanked the ancestors deeply for their love, courage, and reverence for the land they lived on and to forge ahead to make a better world for me. Native Americans say that within a person we each carry the wounds and wisdom of seven generations back and we push forward for seven generations those we hold in our beingness. These ancestors thanked me deeply for doing the work I was doing, for I was healing many of the wounds and traumas around love and fear that have been generationally carried forward. I was extremely humbled to be doing this work and so grateful to be able to provide those spirits with healing, which would enable them to travel the spirit world, or return to this world, more free and full of love.

As the night continued, I would see a light off in a corner that would bring about a brightness to the room I can't explain. Author, indigenous soul seeker, and Mayan Shaman Martín Prechtel writes of how we live in a kind of a dark age, craftily lit with synthetic light, so that no one can tell how dark it has really gotten for our world these days. In this room with the light, I sensed another world coming to me and letting me know I am being watched and cared for. Furthermore, throughout the night I would sense a grandfather elder sitting in the empty leather chair behind me smoking a tobacco pipe and blowing the smoke on me as he offered up prayers and healing. His smoke penetrated the air and I knew he was there, even if I could not see him. This night there were ancestors all around me, healing me and teaching me how to be nourished in a new, loving way.

In the vastness of this evening, I came to see—to experience—how enormous love is and how hard it can be to receive it. I recognized that love, just like surrender, is not about a state of willing, giving, or doing. But rather it is a reverent state of being in every moment, every aspect of one's life. I do not love another, I am love and I am the other, there are no boundaries between you, me, and love. We are all one and the same amongst all living things.

Chapter 9: What I Learned

We are not what we know, but what we are willing to learn.
– Mary Catherine Bateson

A cultural system an embodiment of the range of activities, social conflicts, and moral dilemmas in which individuals are compelled to engage as they go about negotiating everyday events that confront them in their lives. A collective worldview reflects specific philosophies or belief systems concerning how the world works, the place of humans within it, and thus, how these individuals should live their lives. Our current dominant worldview is called anthropocentrism, that is, our activities and behaviors place humans at the center of this world and a value system that all else exists as utilitarian value for the human consumer experience.

This modern worldview is reflected in those individual decisions and actions we each take as we navigate our daily dilemmas. Behaviors and value systems based on profit, growth, and consumption reflect a worldview that is fundamentally economic in nature. This economic engine, which dominates Western society and the global economy, reflects a belief system that rationalizes that individual acts of self-interest somehow serve the common interests of society as a whole.

If all this were good for us, why are we less satisfied with life despite our growing wealth, financial independence, and increased security? Could it be that happiness pursued through material possessions, indulgence of physical pleasures, and avoidance of sensual pain is not happiness at all, but rather is a distraction from our truer sense of self and collective identity? Could it be that the daily threat of annihilation be it environmental, nuclear, political, financial, or other acts of violence are a result of our anthropocentric lifestyle? Perhaps it is in the dehumanization of a competitive capitalistic society that narrows our vision to material gains and, as a result, we are confused about our true identity in the larger scheme of things and thus unhappy?

Either way, the obvious growing discomfort with our lifestyle is throwing us into an identity crisis of authenticity. While this can be a good catalyst for transformation, we have created defense mechanisms to keep our anxiety at bay through a multitude of distractions such as watching television, using the internet and social media, mobile technology, gaming, alcohol and drug abuse, or "retail therapy." Adding to the ease of distractions around us is the social pressure of conformity and enculturation which provides us an easy escape from our existential quest.

I'm not suggesting we should go back to ancient traditions as they once existed, for they served a different community at a different time. And contemporary America is a secular society that obviously cannot just borrow from these indigenous cultures to heal its own psychic wounds. But the spirit of community healing and connection that forms the basis of these ceremonies is one that a modern society might draw upon. In all cultures, ceremonies are designed to communicate the experience of one group of people to the wider community as a means of learning from one another and deepening our understanding of life. Rather, what I am suggesting is that we hold a sense of curiosity and wonder about what life would look like if we were willing to lean in to learn how these ways shaped and informed us as members of a greater wholeness – perhaps as a reminder that we are part of something greater than just ourselves alone?

Where to Go From Here

Where do we go to safely challenge the worldviews that we each hold individually? How do we begin a journey that starts with our self? How do we show up in the world, individually and collectively? We need to find common ground and then seek out those tools that break down barriers, get people to a shared understanding and united towards a collective goal that benefits the whole of our existence. I found it helpful to ask three central questions, which were originally asked by scholars of the School of Chartres during the Middle Ages:

- How can we, through connection with the spirit, heal the soul?
- How can we, working on the Earth, heal our planet?
- How can we, through a communion in the spirit, heal the body social?

The modern world has long since repressed the notion of rituals and connection to a world that cannot be seen. As bestselling author Yuval Noah Harari comments, "Consumerism and nationalism work extra hours to make us imagine that millions of strangers belong to the same community as ourselves, that we all have a common past, common interests and a common future." It appears that we have managed to make the natural way of living look primitive, full of ignorance and poverty, so that we can appreciate our "enslavement to the corporate machine" as West African Elder and indigenous author Malidoma Somé writes. We make those who are not enslaved feel sorry for themselves, just as I still sometimes feel sorry for myself when people ask me *what do I do* and then take pity upon me, for I do not "work" right now. Without question, this journey and my Ph.D. research is beyond the hardest work I have ever done, regardless of monetary gain.

Many people today find our contemporary way of being frenetic too fast to comprehend, and they are overwhelmed by the mere prospect of living. Worse yet, in our efforts to become more efficient and effective, we have become a singular society, reducing ourselves to a culture of individuals who worship youth and cast aside elders. As a result, many of us have lost our tribe, that community we depend upon, and instead live in emotional and psychological poverty with no one to turn to. We have forgotten that culture completes humanity by explaining and interpreting the world around us, yet left unchecked, culture can also control and forbids us to think and act in certain ways.

We need to find a convergence between emerging thoughts in systems thinking, ecological sustainability, indigenous wisdom, and modern science to find balanced and timely solutions for the challenges of our times. Yet any approach to solving some of our largest social issues today, such as inequality, poverty, racism, or discrimination that fails to engage the human spirit needs to be called into question. It should be obvious that what is needed today is a reorientation of our fear-based, self-centered focused perspective, if fundamental and lasting change is desired. For it is not just our inner afflictions that arise from soul loss; the crises of our outer world can be traced there as well. Wilderness guide and author Bill Plotkin wrote, "When we become alienated from soul—or inner nature—we lose respect for outer nature, resulting in degradation of the whole environment."

To do this, we must find the courage to change ourselves just as our world is ever changing. Rites of passages are one such transformational experience that is designed to hold a person capable of assimilation through their life experiences and the change happening around them. Wilderness guide leader John Davis explained this when he says, "Ultimately, the meaning of a transition is growth, and the archetypal gift—a vision—is what reflects that growth; understanding and celebrating this meaning helps to complete transitions."

Ceremony is one way to help people face up to our human wholeness through the healing it provides for our modern world. These indigenous ways of being that I studied and experienced are intrinsically different, but they universally express common fundamental values such as harmony, diversity, and connection, with oneness of all. However, these views differ greatly from today's notion of development and prosperity, challenging the dogmatic belief that the path toward a better future is through economic growth and profit with an underlying assumption that the wealth of one equals the wealth of many.

Indigenous traditions propose that when individuals or a community becomes too serious, anxious, or are disconnected and grieving in some way, that everyone stops what they are doing and enters into ceremony. It is time we heed this wisdom and step out of the frenetic life we are living, reconnect with one another, and remember ourselves in the world we are a part of, not separate from.

Our awakening, our becoming whole, is not about changing others and it cannot be found in public policy, regulation, environmentalism, or even religion. Becoming whole is not even about changing our self, rather it is about changing our perspective of the world as something external to us and instead realizing we simultaneously co-exist, dependent on each other for our own survival regardless of our color, race, religion, nationality, or species.

What I Learned

On my journey, I realized that the most important part of my living is in my learning how to die. I came to realize that my biggest fear of dying was not in leaving my loved ones, but in how they will remember me when I am gone. It was through the ceremonies that held me safe and guided my transitions through death and rebirth time and again that really taught me how to fully live. Through these ancient rituals, I learned to see how life is not linear but rather dynamic and ever-changing and I must learn to adapt or suffer the dis-ease of being trapped in any one of the four directions. As I traveled around the medicine wheel, I was reminded that my entire life is simultaneously one big pilgrimage with a million smaller ones within, each turn providing profound opportunities for my growth and transformation between my spiritual being (East) and my psychological doing (West) and between the individuality of my physical self (South) fully in communion with the other (North).

From the death of my parents and my husband's illness, to trekking the Himalayas and fasting in the desert, to my latest spiritual deep dives and ayahuasca's love, each experience opened a new door as if to plant a seed for deeper inquiry at just the right time. Mustering up all the courage I could to face my ego deaths, every passage I embarked on was a further pilgrimage into a dis-identification of the world I was *had* by and a re-integration with a new, self-transformed perspective. I realize that I am not, and cannot, be had by anyone out there without my granting them permission first, if only through abdication of my responsibility. I gradually became able to subordinate my old ways of making meaning, of associating and identifying myself through how others saw me, toward one where I could stand in separation from the other's perspective, holding my own while still hearing and responding to the other fully.

As I turned 50, I sought to redefine what it means to be an elder in community as I saw around me how the younger trees grow up near the elders, constantly looking toward them not just for how to live, but even more so for how to die in communion of the whole rather than alone, cast aside as washed-up and no longer of use. In the forest that could never happen. In a forest of trees, life is about living and dying together, in balance. It means co-creating the world around us as we are simultaneously shaping and being shaped by each other every day in a sacred reciprocity of taking to support the self and, in return, giving of the entire self to support the whole. It means being embodied in a dance of love. In a forest, taking for yourself is not selfish when it enables you to fully show up attuned to the whole, able to give of your entire being for the well-being of everything around you. It is only when the individual takes from the community for only the self that disease and sickness begins

Transcending the I

to emerge. Only when one slowly withdraws from the container of the whole does the possibility of a death seeped in depression and isolation emerge, a death very different than dying in community. Alternatively, to live fully in a community you do not die a final death, rather you give of yourself so that you may be held gently in the breast of the collective soul of that community which gave you so much in your life. Members of your community carefully and lovingly take you into their soil so that you may be loved and held as you transition—and like a midwife to mother Earth, they hold you to witness your rebirth.

Carol A. Grojean, M.A., M.B.A., M.S., Ph.D. is a leadership and organizational system social scientist who supports radical leadership and social transformation. Working internationally, Carol guides whole system shifts through building self-authored, adaptive leaders passionate about bringing transformation and peace from within.

More at www.CarolGrojean.com

Made in the USA
Middletown, DE
07 February 2019